SpringerBriefs in Political Science

SpringerBriefs present concise summaries of cutting-edge research and practical applications across a wide spectrum of fields. Featuring compact volumes of 50 to 125 pages, the series covers a range of content from professional to academic. Typical topics might include:

- A timely report of state-of-the art analytical techniques
- A bridge between new research results, as published in journal articles, and a contextual literature review
- A snapshot of a hot or emerging topic
- An in-depth case study or clinical example
- A presentation of core concepts that students must understand in order to make independent contributions

SpringerBriefs in Political Science showcase emerging theory, empirical research, and practical application in political science, policy studies, political economy, public administration, political philosophy, international relations, and related fields, from a global author community.

SpringerBriefs are characterized by fast, global electronic dissemination, standard publishing contracts, standardized manuscript preparation and formatting guidelines, and expedited production schedules.

Jasmin Dall'Agnola · Aijan Sharshenova
Editors

Researching Central Asia

Navigating Positionality in the Field

Editors
Jasmin Dall'Agnola ⓘ
The Institute for European,
Russian and Eurasian Studies
The George Washington University
Washington, DC, USA

Aijan Sharshenova ⓘ
OSCE Academy in Bishkek
Bishkek, Kyrgyzstan

ISSN 2191-5466 ISSN 2191-5474 (electronic)
SpringerBriefs in Political Science
ISBN 978-3-031-39023-4 ISBN 978-3-031-39024-1 (eBook)
https://doi.org/10.1007/978-3-031-39024-1

© The Editor(s) (if applicable) and The Author(s) 2024. This book is an open access publication.

Open Access This book is licensed under the terms of the Creative Commons Attribution 4.0 International License (http://creativecommons.org/licenses/by/4.0/), which permits use, sharing, adaptation, distribution and reproduction in any medium or format, as long as you give appropriate credit to the original author(s) and the source, provide a link to the Creative Commons license and indicate if changes were made.
The images or other third party material in this book are included in the book's Creative Commons license, unless indicated otherwise in a credit line to the material. If material is not included in the book's Creative Commons license and your intended use is not permitted by statutory regulation or exceeds the permitted use, you will need to obtain permission directly from the copyright holder.
The use of general descriptive names, registered names, trademarks, service marks, etc. in this publication does not imply, even in the absence of a specific statement, that such names are exempt from the relevant protective laws and regulations and therefore free for general use.
The publisher, the authors, and the editors are safe to assume that the advice and information in this book are believed to be true and accurate at the date of publication. Neither the publisher nor the authors or the editors give a warranty, expressed or implied, with respect to the material contained herein or for any errors or omissions that may have been made. The publisher remains neutral with regard to jurisdictional claims in published maps and institutional affiliations.

This Springer imprint is published by the registered company Springer Nature Switzerland AG
The registered company address is: Gewerbestrasse 11, 6330 Cham, Switzerland

Note on Transliteration

All Kazakh and Russian terms and phrases are rendered in English. Transliteration from Kazakh[1] and Russian[2] is based on the Library of Congress system, whereby 'я' is rendered as 'ia' except at the beginning of a word, where it has been written as 'ya' for greater readability. Also, for reasons of accessibility to non-Russian/Kazakh speakers, the soft sign has been connoted by a single apostrophe, except in proper names, where it has been dropped. All names of Kazakh political actors and places are transliterated as indicated by official governmental online sources such as https://www.akorda.kz/en. For example, the president of Kazakhstan is spelled Kassym-Jomart Tokayev rather than Kassym-Zhomart Tokayev in this book. All foreign words are *italicised* with the exception of proper names.

---

[1] https://www.loc.gov/catdir/cpso/romanization/kazakh.pdf (last accessed January 10, 2023).
[2] https://www.loc.gov/catdir/cpso/romanization/russian.pdf (las accessed January 10, 2023).

Contents

1 **The Central Asian Research Setting: An Introduction** 1
   Jasmin Dall'Agnola and Aijan Sharshenova

Part I Epistemic and Methodological Uncertainty

2 **Making Sense of Central Asia Sources of Epistemic
   Uncertainty** 11
   Aziz Elmuradov

3 **Pitfalls and Promise for Public Opinion Research in Central
   Asia** 19
   Kasiet Ysmanova

4 **'Swiping Right'—The Ethics of Using Tinder as a Recruitment
   Tool in the Field** 27
   Paolo Sorbello

Part II Beyond 'Outsiders' and 'Locals'

5 **The Power of a Multi-layered Identity in Central
   Asian Research** 37
   Gulzhanat Gafu

6 **Being Afghani, French and not Soviet Along the Border Between
   Tajikistan and Afghanistan** 47
   Mélanie Sadozaï

7 **A Stranger in the Village: Anti-blackness in the Field** 57
   Alexa Kurmanov

Part III Doing Research in Closed Contexts

8 **Safety, Security, and Self-Censorship as Survival Strategies** 67
   Aijan Sharshenova

9	**Navigating Academic Repression in Central Asia** 77
	Ruslan Norov
10	**Performative Heterosexuality: A Gay Researcher Doing Fieldwork in Central Asia** 87
	Marius Honig
11	**From Romantic Advances to Cyberstalking in the Field** 97
	Jasmin Dall'Agnola

Editors and Contributors

About the Editors

Jasmin Dall'Agnola is a postdoctoral Visiting Scholar at the George Washington University's Elliott School of International Affairs Institute for European, Russian and Eurasian Studies. She holds a Ph.D. in Politics and International Relations from Oxford Brookes University. Her research focuses on the relationship between technology, surveillance and governance in authoritarian societies. Her research has been published in numerous peer-reviewed academic journals, including *Europe-Asia Studies*, *Religions*, *Central Asian Affairs, Surveillance & Society* and *Central Asian Survey*. She is the Lead Editor of the book, *Researching the Former Soviet Union: Stories From the Field* (Routledge, 2023).

Aijan Sharshenova is a Bishkek-based political Analyst and a Research Fellow at the Foreign Policy Centre in London and the European Neighbourhood Council in Brussels. She holds a Ph.D. in Politics awarded at the University of Leeds, UK. In addition to her academic background in international studies, she has worked at the UN and UNDP country offices in the Middle East. Her research interests include foreign policy, public diplomacy, democracy promotion, autocracy diffusion in Russia and Central Asia.

Contributors

Jasmin Dall'Agnola The George Washington University, Washington, DC, USA

Aziz Elmuradov Bielefeld University, Bielefeld, Germany

Gulzhanat Gafu Nazarbayev University, Astana, Kazakhstan

Marius Honig Iserlohn, Germany

Alexa Kurmanov University of California, Berkeley, CA, USA

Ruslan Norov Stockholm, Sweden

Mélanie Sadozaï George Washington University, Washington, DC, USA; INALCO/Sorbonne Paris Cité, Paris, France

Aijan Sharshenova OSCE Academy Bishkek, Bishkek, Kyrgyzstan

Paolo Sorbello Ca' Foscari University of Venice, Venezia, Italy

Kasiet Ysmanova Central Asia Barometer, Bishkek, Kyrgyzstan

Chapter 1
The Central Asian Research Setting: An Introduction

Jasmin Dall'Agnola and Aijan Sharshenova

Abstract Researching Central Asia can be interesting, entertaining, life-changing, traumatising and, at the very least, thought provoking. The way we, Central Asians and Central Asianists, experience the region differs, but it certainly impacts our lives in a multitude of small and not-so-small ways. In this chapter, the editors reflect on the reasons why the Central Asian research setting has become more popular, and what this means both for individual researchers and the study area in general. The need to systematise and structure the diverse experiences of insiders and outsiders, the attraction of the region against the background of Russia's invasion of Ukraine, as well as the ongoing discussions of Russian colonialism and decolonisation in Central Asia have all contributed to the urgency of this book.

Keywords Central Asia · Research Methods · Ethics · Decolonization · Positionality

The idea for this volume emerged during a post-COVID-19 lunch gathering in a coffee shop in Bishkek. While exchanging anecdotes about conducting research in and on Central Asia, we both noticed that there were realms of literature on fieldwork in Central Asia (Heathershaw & Mullojonov, 2020; Koch, 2013; Lottholz, 2018; Thibault, 2021; Wood, 2023), but the image they painted of their field did not always mirror our experiences. Of the handful of scholars who have written openly about the unique obstacles that the Central Asian research setting presents to researchers, the advice they gave was only partially applicable in our cases. Previous scholarship has highlighted that field research is an area not yet comprehensively addressed in conversations on diversity and equity in the academic and non-academic profession

J. Dall'Agnola (✉)
The George Washington University, Washington, DC, USA
e-mail: jasmin.dallagnola@gwu.edu

A. Sharshenova
OSCE Academy Bishkek, Bishkek, Kyrgyzstan
e-mail: a.sharshenova@osce-academy.net

© The Author(s) 2024
J. Dall'Agnola and A. Sharshenova (eds.), *Researching Central Asia*, SpringerBriefs in Political Science, https://doi.org/10.1007/978-3-031-39024-1_1

within Central Asia (Collins et al., 2023; Janenova, 2019; Kudaibergenova, 2019; Marat & Aisarina, 2021; Suyarkulova, 2019). It is the intersectionality of various categories of differences—age, gender, race, sexuality, education, class, parental status and religious practices that not only "shape researchers' [and practitioners'] access to the field but also how they are received by their informants and the local society" (Dall'Agnola, 2023a, 12). A researcher's positionality results in different expectations, risks and dilemmas in the field.

While we have learned from, and draw on the recent literature, it still consists largely of individual experiences, placed side by side rather than in conversation with each other. Through the medium of first-hand accounts of field research in and on Central Asia, this edited volume seeks to address this gap in the literature. It discusses the discrepancies between textbook advice and the reality in the field observed by both non- and local scholars and practitioners in Central Asia. As such, the chapters present an honest and reflective selection of accounts of the authors' personal experience in the Central Asian research setting. Moreover, the scope of this book is not only situated in the range of geographical countries under analysis (e.g. Kazakhstan, Kyrgyzstan, Tajikistan, Turkmenistan and Uzbekistan), but also the contributors represent various disciplines in the industry (e.g. journalism, opinion polling, NGOs), social sciences (e.g. anthropology, political science, education), genders, nationalities, and are affiliated with numerous institutions in different parts of the world. By featuring an even greater variety of academic and non-academic voices, this volume therefore fills an important gap in the literature on fieldwork and knowledge production in and on Central Asia.

A second trigger for writing the book is the growing number of Russophone researchers who, due to the inaccessibility of Russia, Belarus and Ukraine following the Russian invasion of Ukrainian territory in February 2022, are drawn to the (former) Russian-speaking countries of Central Asia that are now considered to be more 'accessible' and 'safe'. Both assumptions are uninformed and highly problematic. Access to the different Central Asian countries is anything but straightforward and varies depending on the researcher and practitioner's positionality, as the personal reflections in this book demonstrate. Furthermore, Russophone scholars' presumption that the Central Asian research setting is 'safe' is deceptive. Scholars and their collaborators, whether local or non-local, suspected of government critique can be monitored, arrested, intimidated and forced out of the country, as the contributions in this edited volume highlight. Moreover, we agree with Marat and Kassymbekova (2023, 10) that "decolonising Central Asian studies involves decentring Russia in understanding the area". Central Asia may share "a history of Russian occupation", but we should stop studying the region through a Russian lens. The personal stories presented in this volume outline some of the unique ethical, structural and methodological obstacles that scholars and practitioners from various social and institutional backgrounds face when conducting research in and on Central Asia, obstacles which are often not encountered in other countries formerly occupied by Soviet Russia.

A final consideration for writing this book is the on-going discussion among Central Asian experts around the need to decolonise the knowledge production in and on Central Asia. As is openly and honestly revealed in this collection through personal stories, research in the Central Asian states of Kazakhstan, Kyrgyzstan, Tajikistan, Turkmenistan and Uzbekistan, can involve several unexpected dangers and risks for both research participants and fieldworkers. The pitfalls and risks scholars face vary depending on their positionality in the field. Yet, researchers' identities and relations to the field are a bit more varied than the stereotypical dichotomy of westerners and locals for whom the field is their "home", "battlefield" and "livelihood" (Kudaibergenova, 2019) would suggest. We appreciate where our authors are living and working, but their identities and lived experiences are a little bit more complex than their passports and institutional affiliations suggest. Half of our authors were born and raised in Central Asia and the other half has spent a significant amount of time living and conducting research in and on the region. And again, others are locals, but a different kind of "local". The fact that some of our contributors are now affiliated to an institution outside of their home country reflects not only the difficulty of undertaking research into sensitive or taboo topics for academics in authoritarian contexts (Glasius et al., 2018), but also the political economy of academia and academic migration flows more widely (Burlyuk & Rahbari, 2023). This in itself reveals something about local researchers' knowledge production and lived experiences in the Central Asian research context. Finally, we are convinced that to diversify and enhance the scholarship on fieldwork and positionality in the region, we need contributions from both local and non-local researchers—with discussion of the wider politics of allyship within academia.

The book is composed of 10 in-depth case studies from the Central Asian region. Some chapters are based on contributors' research experiences in a single Central Asian country, while others are comparative and cut across the region. Each chapter deals with a different topic related to their work in the region. While documenting this subject, the authors engage with their positionality and intersectional identity and offer useful guidance for other scholars and practitioners researching the region. The volume consists of three thematic sections. In the remainder of this introductory chapter, we present the three key themes that emerged from the various personal stories in this volume.

Epistemic and Methodological Uncertainty

Section one (*Epistemic and Methodological Uncertainty*) presents personal accounts that seek to problematise and reconceptualise the epistemology and methodology researchers use to study Central Asia. As such, the authors propose useful tips and recommendations for companies and scholars that plan to conduct research in and on the region. In his opening chapter, Aziz Elmuradov discusses the role of academic positionality in the context of fast-evolving Central Asian scholarship. He argues that a sense of epistemic uncertainty is a concomitant effect of academic positionality and that it may arise at the cross-roads of various cognitive and affective modes and templates. In Chapter three, Kasiet Ysmanova outlines the methodological and political uncertainty local opinion polling companies are confronted with when collecting public opinion data across the region. She argues that Central Asian authorities' censorship of survey research is another significant impediment to local scholarship and as such, to hearing Central Asian voices. She finds that the use of phone polls can help survey companies to circumvent respondents' self-censorship and desirability biases in an authoritarian context. However, it is not only opinion polling centres that increasingly rely on digital technologies to recruit interview participants, as Paolo Sorbello's account in chapter four suggests. Zooming in on how social media and dating platforms can facilitate participant recruitment in Central Asia, he discusses how Tinder helped him to recruit women working in Kazakhstan's oil sector, who under less informal circumstances would not have agreed to talk to him. Sorbello concludes that the use of 'unconventional apps', such as Tinder, for recruiting sources for research is a possibility that can and should be exploited in contexts where informal contacts are more customary.

Beyond 'Outsiders' and 'Locals'

When reflecting on their fieldwork experiences, scholars tend to fall into thinking in terms of a stereotypical dichotomy: western researchers, who go to visit them, the local scholars, in their field (Glasius et al., 2018). The personal stories in the second part of this volume (*Beyond 'Outsiders' and 'Locals'*) challenge this stereotypical dichotomy. They show that 'locals' are not invariably 'rooted' to and Westerners are not invariably 'detached' from the soil of the field. In Chapter five, Gulzhanat Gafu reflects on how her studies abroad influenced the way in which she researches her home country's higher education system, in her case Kazakhstan. Her personal story shows that it is not solely Western researchers, but also local scholars' class and institutional privileges that influence their access to the field. As such, she refashions our understanding of what it means to be a local to the region where someone conducts research, and who is also a western-educated "inbetweener" (Milligan, 2016, 248). While Gafu's institutional affiliation marked her out as a 'privileged' outsider, Mélanie Sadozaï, ostensibly a 'westerner' with her French passport, was identified by her respondents along the border between Tajikistan and Afghanistan as an insider thanks to her Afghani roots. In Chapter six, Sadozaï shows how her personal ties to Badakhshan facilitated deep and rich reflections from her interviewees and marked her out not 'just as a foreigner'. For some scholars, it is not only their passport, but also their physical appearance that makes them an outsider in the eyes of their interlocutors. This is something, Alexa Kurmanov, a black queer scholar researching Kyrgyzstan knows too well. Yet, Kurmanov is not only an outsider in her field side, but also in her home country, the United States. In her chapter (chapter seven), she discusses the ways her black non-binary body becomes fatigued at the intersections of blackness and sexuality in the context of contemporary Kyrgyzstan and her home country. She finds that academic institutions in the United States are

1 The Central Asian Research Setting: An Introduction   5

still failing to identify 'Black fatigue' as an outcome of mundane encounters in fieldwork and Western academia more generally.

Doing Research in Closed Contexts

The final part of this volume (*Doing Research in Closed Contexts*) homes in on the survival strategies employed by both local and non-local Central Asian scholars when conducting fieldwork in the more closely monitored societies of Central Asia (Dall'Agnola, 2023b). In reflecting on their research experiences in a field under authoritarianism, they offer insights for other researchers on how to maximise their own physical safety and mental well-being prior to, during and after fieldwork. In her piece, Chapter eight, Aijan Sharshenova discusses the intangible fear of every Central Asian political scientist, mainly being prosecuted for writing critically about politics in an increasingly political tense environment. In her contribution, Aijan focusses on tangible threats and intangible fears experienced by political scientists, observers, commenters and others, who have to walk a fine line between doing their job in an open and honest manner, and keeping themselves and their families safe. Likewise, in being honest and transparent about his experiences with the secret service in his former Central Asian home country, Ruslan Norov's personal account in Chapter nine details how state monitoring can not only affect local scholars' knowledge production but can also force them to leave their country out of fear of being jailed and prosecuted for being a Western spy. Both Sharshenova and Norov's accounts emphasise that state shadowing of local academics and practitioners does not necessarily stop when the research project comes to an end. Central Asian governments are known for monitoring both the offline and online realms by means of digital technologies (Dall'Agnola, 2023b).

Likewise, foreign fieldworkers can be the target of wiretapping and malware, and find their own and their respondents' privacy and anonymity intruded upon (Dall'Agnola, 2023b). As such, digital surveillance has becomes a permanent feature of both local and Western scholars' life due to their long-lasting involvement in the region. Especially LGBTQ + researchers are forced to silence their sexuality in both their off- and online presence to protect themselves from physical and mental harm, as the personal account of Marius Honig demonstrates. In Chapter ten, he reflects on the limited choices available to LGBTQ + researchers to protect themselves and the limitations of performing a heterosexual male identity in the Central Asian research context. Finally, digital technologies can also be used by respondents to monitor and harass scholars on the Internet and social media long after they have left the field. In her closing chapter, Jasmin Dall'Agnola discusses the implications of unwanted sexual advances and cyberstalking on women scholars' personal and professional life. She argues that some Central Asian men continued their unwanted advances online through the Internet long after she had returned to her home country. Dall'Agnola's story illustrates the harmful influence that interlocutors (and especially local men) can have on female fieldworkers. In critically reflecting about both the level of sexual harassment and violence against women in Switzerland and Central Asia, Dall'Agnola asks us to not forget that violence against women is a problem both in the Central Asian and Western context.

Concluding Remarks

Given the rich detail and insightful reflections in this volume, it is our hope that this book will contribute to improving the practice of fieldwork and other research activities in Central Asia, by laying bare some of the dilemmas and trade-offs scholars and practitioners may (or may not) encounter when conducting research in and on the region. Not every researcher will experience the same ethical, personal or methodological challenges as those outlined here. Still, the chapters offer insights into how those concerned adapted when facing adversity and unforeseen dilemmas. We hope this will aid other researchers in thinking about how they might also approach, cope with and even avoid similar situations. As such, we hope that this book will be a useful teaching tool in pre-fieldwork courses.

Furthermore, the personal stories presented in this collection demonstrate that we need more honest reflections on potentially uncomfortable and sensitive themes that are too little discussed, let alone written about in the academic and professional realm: researchers' fears, insecurities and mistakes during fieldwork, the mental impact it has on the researcher, and the possibility of coming home with little in the way of publishable findings. We hope that the reflections in this book will invite further academic discussion about researchers' unspoken challenges and issues when conducting research in the region. Finally, beyond the academy, we expect some personal accounts in this book to make useful readings for policymakers, civil society practitioners, businesspeople or journalists who find themselves in the Central Asian research setting or dealing with Central Asian state authorities.

References

Burlyuk, O., & Rahbari, L. (2023). *Migrant academics' narratives of precarity and resilience in Europe*. Open Book Publishers. https://doi.org/10.11647/OBP.0331

Collins, N., Sharplin, E., & Burkhanov, A. (2023). Challenges for political science research ethics in autocracies: A case study of Central Asia. *Political Studies Review*. https://doi.org/10.1177/14789299231153074.

Dall'Agnola, J. (2023a). The challenges of fieldwork in post-soviet societies. In J. Dall'Agnola, A. Edwards, & M. Howlett (Eds.), *Researching in the former soviet union. stories from the field* (pp. 1–16). BASEES/Routledge Series on Russian and East European Studies. https://doi.org/10.4324/9781003144168-1.

Dall'Agnola, J. (2023b). Fieldwork under surveillance: A research note. *Surveillance & Society, 21*(2), https://doi.org/10.24908/ss.v21i2.16455

Glasius, M., de Lange, M., Bartman, J., Dalmasso, E., Lv, A., Del Sordi, A., Michaelsen, M., & Ruijgrok, K. (2018). *Research, ethics and risk in the authoritarian field*. Palgrave Macmillan.

Heathershaw, J., & Mullojonov, P. (2020). The politics and ethics of fieldwork in post-conflict environments: The dilemmas of a vocational approach. In B. Bliesemann de Guevara & M. Bøås (Eds.), *Doing fieldwork in areas of international intervention: A guide to research in violent and closed contexts* (pp. 93–112). Bristol University Press. https://doi.org/10.46692/9781529206913.007

Koch, N. (2013). Introduction—Field methods in 'closed contexts': Undertaking research in authoritarian states and places. *Area, 45*(4), 390–395. https://doi.org/10.1111/area.12044

Janenova, S. (2019). The boundaries of research in an authoritarian state. *International Journal of Qualitative Methods, 18*, 1–8. https://doi.org/10.1177/1609406919876469

Kudaibergenova, D. (2019, October 7). When your field is also your home: Introducing feminist subjectivities in Central Asia. *openDemocracy*. https://www.opendemocracy.net/en/odr/when-your-field-also-your-home-introducing-feminist-subjectivities-central-asia/

Lottholz, P. (2018). Researcher safety in peace, conflict and security studies in Central Asia and beyond: Making sense and finding new ways forward. *Security Praxis* (pp. 1–7).

Marat, E., & Aisarina, Z. (2021, January 8). Towards a more equal field in Central Asia research. *openDemocracy* https://www.opendemocracy.net/en/odr/towards-more-equal-field-central-asia-research/

Marat, E., & Kassymbekova, B. (2023). Reclaiming the narrative: Decolonising Central Asian studies for a more inclusive understanding. *APSA Comparative Politics Newsletter, 33*(1), 9–12. https://www.comparativepoliticsnewsletter.org/wp-content/uploads/2023/05/APSA-CP_May_2023.pdf

Milligan, L. (2016). Insider-Outsider-Inbetweener? Researcher positioning, participative methods and cross-cultural educational research. *Compare: A Journal of Comparative and International Education, 46*(2), 235–250. https://doi.org/10.1080/03057925.2014.928510

Suyarkulova, M. (2019, October 10). A view from the margins: Alienation and accountability in Central Asian studies. *openDemocracy*. https://www.opendemocracy.net/en/odr/view-margins-alienation-and-accountability-central-asian-studies/

Thibault, H. (2021). 'Are you married?': Gender and faith in political ethnographic research. *Journal of Contemporary Ethnography, 50*(3), 395–416. https://doi.org/10.1177/0891241620986852

Wood, C. (2023). Listening and its limits: Reflections on fieldwork in/on Kyrgyzstan. In J. Dall'Agnola, A. Edwards, & M. Howlett (Eds.), *Researching in the former soviet union. stories from the field* (pp. 111–127). BASEES/Routledge Series on Russian and East European Studies. https://doi.org/10.4324/9781003144168-10

Jasmin Dall'Agnola is a postdoctoral Visiting Scholar at the George Washington University's Elliott School of International Affairs Institute for European, Russian and Eurasian Studies. She holds a PhD in Politics and International Relations from Oxford Brookes University. Her research focuses on the relationship between technology, surveillance and governance in authoritarian societies. Her research has been published in numerous peer-reviewed academic journals, including *Europe-Asia Studies, Central Asian Affairs, Central Asian Survey* and *Surveillance & Society*. She is the Lead Editor of the book, Researching the Former Soviet Union: Stories From the Field (Routledge, 2023).

Aijan Sharshenova is a Bishkek-based political Analyst and a Research Fellow at the Foreign Policy Centre in London and the European Neighbourhood Council in Brussels. She holds a PhD in Politics awarded at the University of Leeds, UK. In addition to her academic background in international studies, she has worked at the UN and UNDP country offices in the Middle East. Her research interests include foreign policy, public diplomacy, democracy promotion, autocracy diffusion in Russia and Central Asia.

Open Access This chapter is licensed under the terms of the Creative Commons Attribution 4.0 International License (http://creativecommons.org/licenses/by/4.0/), which permits use, sharing, adaptation, distribution and reproduction in any medium or format, as long as you give appropriate credit to the original author(s) and the source, provide a link to the Creative Commons license and indicate if changes were made.

The images or other third party material in this chapter are included in the chapter's Creative Commons license, unless indicated otherwise in a credit line to the material. If material is not included in the chapter's Creative Commons license and your intended use is not permitted by statutory regulation or exceeds the permitted use, you will need to obtain permission directly from the copyright holder.

Part I
Epistemic and Methodological Uncertainty

Chapter 2
Making Sense of Central Asia Sources of Epistemic Uncertainty

Aziz Elmuradov

Abstract Central Asia is in flux, and so are the perspectives and angles of intellectual inquiry, as are the modes of and approaches to the scientific investigation of the region. This paper sets out to discuss the role of academic positionality essential to this flux—caught between modernity and tradition—and reflects on one of its striking effects, epistemic ambiguity. In light of knowledge-related turns in the social sciences, notably, the epistemological twists and turns entailed in postmodernist, postcolonial, decolonial, and feminist critique, the study of academic positionality and its implications in the Central Asian context is a worthwhile pursuit.

Keywords Central Asia · Epistemic uncertainty · Tradition · Local epistemologies · Decolonial critique · Geopolitics of knowledge

Introduction

In bringing to the fore the topic of academic positionality in Central Asia, the editors of this volume have undertaken a worthwhile, exciting, and timely endeavor. There are a great many reasons in view of which inquiring into academic positionality in Central Asia may be deemed worthwhile and timely—the ontological and epistemological twists and turns of our times, the enduring relevance in research of wider identity issues, and the slow but growing scholarly recognition of individual, personal, and gendered subjectivities faced by local and foreign intellectuals, not to mention the complex moral dilemmas and ethical issues, linguistic barriers, and methodological challenges that researchers face. Academic positionality entails "ethical, personal and methodological dimensions" and is the "intersectionality of various categories of differences" that inform research (Dall'Agnola, 2023, 12). In this contribution, I will share my impression of wandering through some of this rocky terrain, struggling to map out my way across instances of epistemic uncertainty, ambiguity, and anxiety.

A. Elmuradov (✉)
Bielefeld University, Bielefeld, Germany
e-mail: aziz.elmuradov@uni-bielefeld.de

© The Author(s) 2024
J. Dall'Agnola and A. Sharshenova (eds.), *Researching Central Asia*,
SpringerBriefs in Political Science,
https://doi.org/10.1007/978-3-031-39024-1_2

My account, although predicated on subjective judgement and observation, draws on critical literature and unfolds in a narrative style along two broad lines. First, I hold that "tradition," as slippery and confusing as this notion often is, underlies the conditions of knowledge production in Central Asia. Second, that "modernity," an equally confusing and slippery notion, invariably looms large in the background while informing and, in fact, permeating and penetrating our quest for intellectual inquiry on Central Asia in significant ways. In this account, I relate to "tradition" and "modernity" in the sense of postcolonial and decolonial critique, as a background matrix of contesting social reality—conditions of epistemic emergence—against the backdrop of which meaning-making takes place. In linking "tradition" and "modernity" in such loose terms, what I aim to do is not to engage in in-depth definitional or theoretical elaboration of these concepts, but to try to carve out a suitable niche for the reconstruction of an underlying emergent condition that I think pertains, for the lack of a better term, to a sense of epistemic anxiety on behalf of a scholar navigating their positionality in/on Central Asia.

Sources of Epistemic Uncertainty

It seems that underlying the topic of academic positionality is a peculiar unresolved dilemma: it is an empowering merit and at the same time, a potential pitfall. On the one hand, scholars of areas, studies, and sociologists of knowledge are perfectly aware that academic positionality implies some sort of social positionality, that it entails some sort of normative basis, for example, incorporation of local, native, and unfamiliar voices, and their broader representation in order for social sciences to be truly social. The prevailing conventional wisdom seems to have its roots in the idea, and righteously, that it is through the acknowledgment and appreciation of subjectivities, the silenced or the excluded or the oppressed, that knowledge is acquired and validated. On the other hand, scholars of areas studies and sociologists of knowledge are also aware that they depend on preconceived ideas, interpretative frameworks, sophisticated vantage points, analytical tools, and methodologies in order to "explore" their subject matters and contexts. The process of "exploring" the new is then often informed by presumptions and preconceptions, persistent understandings, and established practices that aim to see meaning within clear-cut paradigms and intelligible frameworks. After all, no one would deny that scholars are also human beings and that, as such, they are ultimately embedded in normative values of this or that cultural milieu, social circle, academic community or society, and their conceptual constructs are, in fact, often intelligible within the established intellectual frameworks in which they are used. It is also true that it is often the case that there are significant discrepancies between textbook advice and the reality of the field (Dall'Agnola, 2023). Conditioned by such circumstances, how can we hope to operate in novel terrain with a sense, more or less, of intellectual integrity and certainty? How can we lay claim to valid knowledge, let alone "truth," when we seem to occupy an ambiguous position of being within knowledge, yet simultaneously outside of it?

Multiple streams of critical thought are mindful of the crucial role of epistemic frameworks in asserting, legitimising, and reinforcing structurally privileged modes of knowledge. In particular, postcolonial and decolonial thought and feminist scholarship are acutely aware of the epistemic problems along such dimensions as culture, gender, religion, class, social status, age, and ability, and in terms of whether a researcher is an "insider" or an "outsider," "foreign" or "local" (Dall'Agnola, 2023). Moreover, that "epistemologies of ignorance" follows from our "situatedness as knowers," or "specific aspects of group identities," or that "oppressive systems produce ignorance" is also well known (Alcoff, 2007, 40; Haraway, 1988, 581). Ultimately, such considerations are insinuated with an implicit concern over power, and its use and abuse; and therefore, they are intimately linked with an idea of imminent conflict and violence. What is also implicit in these considerations is a concern over knowledge as power. What kind of epistemic consequences follow from examining the wider implications of knowledge as power? An intellectual is then all too often faced with a self-posed question of the degree to which they are, in fact, knowledgeable, or even worse, whether or they are engaged in "epistemic violence?" Once aware, we understand that epistemic violence may be deeply embedded in our knowledge as well as in the ways through which we strive toward knowledge.

What I strive to pin down here, with apparent difficulty, is a sense of ambivalence, perhaps the futility of scholarly detachment, of non-knowing, of being caught up between various intellectual matrices of knowledge. To demarcate more precisely, it is perhaps useful to describe the phenomenon I am addressing here as an epistemic dilemma, or sociostructurally conditioned epistemic ambivalence. What we know is often shaped by our "social location," or "locus of enunciation" (Grosfoguel, 2007, 213). We always speak from a particular location in the power structures and the problem of social location goes in tandem with academic location. As a social scientist, one is expected to provide, on the one hand, the best possible account of their subject matter (which is usually a complicated embedded social phenomena) as well as, on the other hand, to present a critique and at times even provide proposals, albeit often implicitly and with a certain normative stance, as to how to modify and improve social constellations in reasonable ways. In doing so, one seeks to push forward an informed, impartial, and reasonable position. From this ostensibly impartial position stem optics (of disembodied knowledge) through which local and provincial knowledge is routinely dismissed due to privileging hegemonic epistemic practices. This circumstance arouses a sense of epistemic anxiety over "the geopolitical and body-political location of the subject that speaks" (Grosfoguel, 2007, 213) and poses crucial questions such as "can the subaltern speak?" (Spivak, 1988).

Making Sense of Central Asia

Central Asian research has been in flux in recent years and a fair amount of attention has focused on epistemic awareness and diversity. With "more diverse voices joining Central Asian studies, […] the field is maturing into a more self-aware community" (Marat, 2021, 479). Scholars with critical, feminist, postcolonial, and decolonial leanings have come to increasingly constitute a significant part of this community. By interrogating conventional theoretical underpinnings and raising new epistemological questions, new voices plead for a broader reconceptualization of the field. The critiques have been voiced in terms of problems relating to "knowledge production," "postcolonial deconstruction" (Sultanalieva, 2019), the "ambivalent role of feminist research" (Mamadshoeva, 2019), and "the need to decolonize international relations" in Central Asia (Dadabaev, 2022). Furthermore, it has been noted that a feminist perspective has long been missing in studies of Central Asia (Arystanbek, 2019; Mamadshoeva, 2019). While the scope of the research field has significantly diversified, the main intellectual and ideological positions are still located in the North. By contrast, the subjects to be studied are located in the South. In other words, Central Asian Studies has not epistemologically transcended Eurocentrism; "sense making" and "social sciencing" remain informed by frameworks obscured by "modernizing reason." This state of affairs also concerns, perhaps first and foremost, the study of the role of tradition and traditionality.

Tradition, conceptualized as modernity's otherness, is more than just a discourse of difference and producing meaning (Elmuradov, 2021). Indeed, while a fair amount of attention has been focused on tradition and its meanings in the Central Asian context (Beyer & Finke, 2019), little attention has been paid to exploring its epistemic implications. It is clear that the concept of tradition does not entail an obvious, fixed, or clear-cut meaning. On the contrary, since tradition hinges on the realm of the social, its manifestations are more fluid and dynamic than is commonly assumed. Tradition entails active elements of social creation and invention. "Tradition is not an object of fixed history but a part of a process of identity formation," and we should regard tradition as "an interpretative concept, not a descriptive one" (Beyer & Finke, 2019, 314). Tradition is then inseparable from the present and "to do something because it is traditional is to reinterpret it, to change it" (Anttonen, 2016, 35). Such explanations are predicated on the idea of tradition as a subject of study and phenomenon of interest. However, what I find most interesting is the epistemic consequences arising from the lived experience of tradition, the manifestations of tradition that are held up as expressions of local knowledge in their own right—experience-based knowledge. While there is ample amount of research on tradition as a subject of inquiry, there is strikingly little research on tradition as an expression of local knowledge. With a few exceptions, most studies focus on interpreting social agents and relations rather than interpreting the world with them and from their perspectives. However, to avoid a possible misunderstanding, it should be made clear that I do not intend to offer a neutral account or an objective representation of what I call the lived experience of tradition as local expressions of knowledge, or experience-based knowledge.

Defining experience-based knowledge is not a value-free endeavor that follows a universal logic, and the question of which "experiences" and what "expressions of knowledge" constitute tradition is always and inevitably the result of a selective perspective.

In Central Asia, experience-based local epistemologies may comprise communal beliefs, cosmologies, rituals, practices, and worldviews, mainly emanating from the high degree of religiosity, the significant role of Islam, the relatively high degree of traditionality in general, and an affinity towards mysterious phenomena. Awareness of local epistemologies may present a crucial opportunity to gain a vivid glimpse of special circumstances and settings. Experience-based local epistemologies put forward "an argument for situated and embodied knowledge and argument against various forms of unlocatable, and so irresponsible, knowledge claims" (Haraway, 1988, 583). As observed by Haraway, "we are bound to seek perspective from those points of view, which can never be known in advance, that promise something quite extraordinary, that is, knowledge potent for constructing worlds less organized by axes of domination" (Haraway, 1988, 585). One of the fundamental tasks in Central Asian Studies today is this: to look for ways of offering better accounts of traditions and customs as local epistemologies.

Grappling with Obstacles

On the other hand, however, there may lie an imminent danger of romanticizing local epistemologies. To see from a local position is neither easy nor unproblematic. We cannot present local epistemologies as if they were a site of pristine and flawless knowledge. Far from being apolitical, tradition as a local epistemology is equally implicated in concerns over the question of power, its use, and abuse. Appeals to tradition sometimes do serve to disguise deeper societal problems. For example, in the Central Asian countries of Uzbekistan, Kyrgyzstan, and Tajikistan, there is a growing trend toward beliefs, practices, and worldviews that emanate from an affinity for religiosity and a proclivity towards recitals of good and evil through telling of religious and quasi-religious narratives and tales, etc. The rise in religiosity is a case in point: conservative moods and sentiments circulate widely, predominantly among the male population. The conservative segments of society employ, in particular, discursive repertoires and strategies to articulate the sociocultural boundaries of the traditional in which they resort to "politics of knowledge": contemplations on the "great past" and moral and ethical values, often propped up by patriotic rhetoric and moralizing religious critique. Even on social media platforms, conservative moods, and trends have gained increasing prominence.

In Uzbekistan, for example, the nascent public domain is just beginning to evolve and is not amply cultivated for discourse through meaningful, consensus-oriented communication. It is true that the coexistence of traditional and modern socialization models and value systems is common to Uzbek society in which a number of social, political, cultural, and religious features intermingle against the background of traditional, Soviet, and modern elements. However, the traditionalist turn is on an upward trend in which appeal to the "age-old traditions" and "true faith" has become a vibrant part of the public imagination and a ready-made point of reference for actors who aspire to redefine the social order in their own interests. In spite of the fact that tradition is an inherently ambivalent phenomenon, it is presented as something that should ensure the continuity of communal practices and impart an idea of stability. Traditional societies have been regarded as being characterized by powerful collective memories that are sanctioned by ritual, with social guardians ensuring the continuity of communal practices (Giddens, 1994, 63–65). Patterns of traditional "stability" and "continuity" are predominantly masculine and, as such, masculine sociabilities are implicated in local power games. A vivid example is the growing affinity for religious and quasi-religious narratives, which are embedded in their own matrix of power.

While reputable scholarly research in the past has meant abstaining from making value judgments, both at home and in the field, today, intellectuals are well aware that detachment is ultimately impossible since knowledge is conceived to exist in direct relationship with power. The knowing subject is caught up within epistemic entanglements of modernity and tradition. This curious circumstance of ambivalence carries profound implications: the inquiring subject is situated, simultaneously, within the multiplicity of perspectives across power-differentiated communities: particular epistemic discourses, ways of experiencing, knowing, speaking, making sense, and representing. In the words of Rosi Braidotti, following Deleuze and Guattari, the inquiring subject is, at the same, time an affective transversal subject (Braidotti, 2019). While modernity has traditionally meant the questioning of authority, the established ways, power and domination, the traditional locus of enunciation has postulated, across many of the Central Asian renderings, the Law of the Father. "You are not to get on the roof of the house where your father is," an Uzbek saying goes. Our "concepts are not part of free-floating philosophical discourse, but socially, historically and locally rooted, and must be explained in terms of these realities" (Hobsbawm, 1990, 9). Notions such as "knowledge," "law," "just society," and "gender" are not just self-evident universal signifiers one can look up in the dictionary, they are locally produced understandings that are rooted in their own matrix of power. Particularly for "outsider" researchers, but also for "insiders," as well as for female researchers, it is immensely difficult to navigate across the site. Circumstances may turn out to be advantageous as often as unfavorable for "outsider" researchers. Traditional accounts of knowledge claim that knowledge emerges from an experiential basis that is subjective and that those who lack subjectivities may not always be able to share that knowledge to its fullest extent. The outsiders may not have sufficient foundation from which to evaluate local knowledge. In short, since reality is socially mediated, it is put forward that only those who belong to a particular setting can know about it and relate to it.

Conclusion

Navigating across Central Asian intellectual terrain engenders a set of epistemic uncertainties induced by a demand for "disembodied scientific objectivity" and "embodied and located knowledge." We have to insist on better accounts and offer critical and reflexive insights into symbolic entanglements of modernity and tradition. As I discussed elsewhere (Elmuradov, 2021), no other analogy could perhaps be more useful in elucidating symbolic entanglements in the discourse of modernity and tradition than reference to the metaphorical figure of Lady Justice—the ultimate allegorical representation of the modern philosophy of law and of equality before the law, the individual, and the idea of the subject. Taken together, the objects she commands represent the conceptual ideal of modernity. The blindfold, scales, and sword epitomize the self-evidence of the supreme authority of truth, with justice applied impartially and objectively. As alluring as her imagery is—femininity, outstanding credentials, and a proven track record of success—the question we must ask is how she might gain a genuinely central position in the discourse in a society that is rooted in multiple, sometimes uneasy, and certainly not always self-evident notions of truth, and one that, to an uncommon degree, is governed by a sense of masculinity. Ironically, despite being physically present as a common sight on the facades of courthouses and legal institutions, it seems justified to enquire to what extent this imagery is, in fact, present in mental frames. Critical reflection on such entanglements pertains to how we make sense of a host of questions in Central Asian studies and how we redefine academic positionality as a medium in reconciling the resulting discrepancies.

References

Alcoff, L. (2007). Epistemologies of ignorance: Three types. In S. Sullivan & N. Tuana (Eds.), *Race and epistemologies of ignorance* (pp. 39–50). State University of New York Press.
Anttonen, P. (2016). *Tradition through modernity: Postmodernism and the nation-state in folklore scholarship*. Finnish Literature Society.
Arystanbek, A. (2019, December 20). Central Asian feminists are carving out their space in gender studies. *OpenDemocracy*, https://www.opendemocracy.net/en/odr/central-asian-feminists-are-carving-out-their-space-gender-studies/
Beyer, J., & Finke, P. (2019). Practices of traditionalization in Central Asia. *Central Asian Survey, 38*(3), 310–328. https://doi.org/10.1080/02634937.2019.1636766
Braidotti, R. (2019). A theoretical framework for the critical posthumanities. *Theory, Culture & Society, 36*(6), 31–61. https://doi.org/10.1177/0263276418771486
Dadabaev, T. (2022). *Decolonizing central asian international relations: Beyond empires*. Routledge.
Dall'Agnola, J. (2023). Introduction: The challenges of fieldwork in post-soviet societies. In J. Dall'Agnola, A. Edwards, & M. Howlett (Eds.), *Researching in the former soviet union: Stories from the field*. BASEES/Routledge series on Russian and East European studies.
Elmuradov, A. (2021). Uzbekistan between modernity and tradition: Subject and symbolic order. In C. Pierobon, N. Becker, & S. Schlegel (Eds.), *Central Asian politics and societies between stability and transformation* (pp. 2–16). Nomos.

Giddens, A. (1994). Living in a post-traditional society. In U. Beck, A. Giddens, S. Lash (Eds.), *Reflexive modernization: Politics, tradition and aesthetics in the modern social order*. Stanford University Press.

Grosfoguel, R. (2007). The epistemic decolonial turn. *Cultural Studies, 21*(2–3), 211–223. https://doi.org/10.1080/09502380601162514

Haraway, D. (1988). Situated knowledges: The science question in feminism and the privilege of partial perspective. *Feminist Studies, 14*(3), 575–599. https://doi.org/10.2307/3178066

Hobsbawm, E. (1990). *Nations and nationalism since 1780: Programme, myth, reality*. Cambridge University Press.

Mamadshoeva, D. (2019, October 9). Listening to women's stories: The ambivalent role of feminist research in Central Asia. *OpenDemocracy*. https://www.opendemocracy.net/en/odr/listening-to-womens-stories-the-ambivalent-role-of-feminist-research-in-central-asia/

Marat, E. (2021). Introduction: 30 years of Central Asian studies—The best is yet to come. *Central Asian Survey, 40*(4), 477–482. https://doi.org/10.1080/02634937.2021.1994921

Spivak, G. (1988). Can the subaltern speak? In C. Nelson & L Grossberg (Eds.), *Marxism and the interpretation of culture* (pp. 271–313). University of Illinois. https://doi.org/10.1007/978-3-658-13213-2_84

Sultanalieva, S. (2019, October 8). How does it feel to be studied? A Central Asian perspective. *OpenDemocracy*. https://www.opendemocracy.net/en/odr/how-does-it-feel-be-studied-central-asian-perspective/. Checked on September 27, 2022.

Aziz Elmuradov is a Research Associate at the Department of Politics and Society at the Faculty of Sociology at Bielefeld University. His doctoral thesis investigated the conceptual framework of Russian foreign policy discourse on the EU. His research interests include analysis of post-Soviet transformation processes against the East/West paradigm, political and historical sociology of autocratic politics in Central Asia. Aziz Elmuradov is the Coordinator of the postdoctoral fellowship program 'Institutional Change and Social Practice. Research on the Political System, the Economy and Society in Central Asia and the Caucasus' funded by the Volkswagen Foundation.

Open Access This chapter is licensed under the terms of the Creative Commons Attribution 4.0 International License (http://creativecommons.org/licenses/by/4.0/), which permits use, sharing, adaptation, distribution and reproduction in any medium or format, as long as you give appropriate credit to the original author(s) and the source, provide a link to the Creative Commons license and indicate if changes were made.

The images or other third party material in this chapter are included in the chapter's Creative Commons license, unless indicated otherwise in a credit line to the material. If material is not included in the chapter's Creative Commons license and your intended use is not permitted by statutory regulation or exceeds the permitted use, you will need to obtain permission directly from the copyright holder.

Chapter 3
Pitfalls and Promise for Public Opinion Research in Central Asia

Kasiet Ysmanova

Abstract The Central Asia Barometer (CAB) is one of the most active opinion polling institutions in Central Asia. It conducts large-scale surveys in all countries of Central Asia, including Turkmenistan. As the director of CAB, I coordinate the groups' various research initiatives, ranging in methodology from phone polls to in-person interviews and focus groups with experts and the wider public. In discussing some of the challenges that my team and I face when collecting public opinion data, I seek to offer useful tips and recommendations for organisations and researchers that plan to conduct public opinion research in Central Asia.

Keywords Opinion polling · Survey research · Authoritarianism · Central Asia

Introduction

Until very recently, only a limited number of public opinion surveys conducted across Central Asia were available to researchers, and those that existed had limited reach, such as the *Life in Kyrgyzstan study* (The Life in Kyrgyzstan Study, 2023), the polls by the International Republic Institute's Centre for Insights in Survey Research (CISR, 2023), the Asia Barometer Survey (2005), or the rounds of World Values Survey (Haerpfer & Kizilova, 2020). These large-scale public opinion surveys often do not cover all five Central Asian countries and are not conducted on a regular basis. In addition, many polls covered only a handful of topics, which were considered safe in light of the political sensitivity in these predominantly autocratic societies; e.g. the *Listening to citizens of Uzbekistan* project (World Bank, 2023), which focusses mostly on economic indicators. Furthermore, most public opinion polls conducted previously in Kazakhstan, Kyrgyzstan and Tajikistan were financed by international organizations (IOs) such as the UN agencies, or by global companies like Coca-Cola.

K. Ysmanova (✉)
Central Asia Barometer, Bishkek, Kyrgyzstan
e-mail: kasiet.ysmanova@ca-barometer.org

© The Author(s) 2024
J. Dall'Agnola and A. Sharshenova (eds.), *Researching Central Asia*,
SpringerBriefs in Political Science,
https://doi.org/10.1007/978-3-031-39024-1_3

Such survey data remains closed to the public due to inertia and lack of incentive on the side of the IOs and global companies.

Since the countries of Central Asia are considered to be more "closed" societies with somewhat backward survey technology (Haerpfer & Kizilova, 2020), most researchers continue to rely on qualitative research methods such as (digital) ethnography, participatory observation, individual interviews and focus groups to obtain up-to-date opinion data from the wider Central Asian public. Recently, however, we are witnessing a growing interest in survey data on Central Asia among both policy analysts and academics. Some researchers are not only using existing survey data in their studies but are also venturing to create their own surveys with the help of local partner organisations such as the Central Asia Barometer (hereafter CAB). CAB is an applied social research centre that conducts opinion polls across the five Central Asian countries of Kazakhstan, Kyrgyzstan, Tajikistan, Turkmenistan and Uzbekistan. It was founded in Bishkek, Kyrgyzstan, by a group of opinion polling enthusiasts in 2012. Since 2017, CAB has organised 13 multiwave public opinion surveys in all five Central Asian countries (CAB, 2023) funded by subscriptions and post-factum purchases of the survey data. CAB's ultimate goal is to run its surveys across the region on a monthly basis and to publish the polling data in a free and open access manner soon after. Currently, CAB only has the means to publish the opinion data in open access format after two years.

In this chapter, I will reflect on my experience in running public opinion polls in my role as the director of CAB. In discussing the challenges that my team and I have encountered when conducting public opinion research in the region, I seek to provide some useful guidance and tips for both organisations and individual scholars that plan to conduct public opinion research in Central Asia. The remainder of this chapter is structured as follows. In the next section, I discuss the various barriers that survey companies and researchers encounter when trying to access Central Asia to conduct public opinion research. I then discuss the mechanisms and methods opinion polling centres have previously adopted in order to run polls on sensitive topics in the region. Finally, I summarise the main takeaways for other scholars and institutes that plan to run public opinion polls in Central Asia.

Entering the Central Asian Field

I would like to start with a very personal observation/statement about the region. Despite their shared historical ties, from my experience working in the opinion polling industry, it is very problematic to assume that public opinion does not vary across the five Central Asian countries of Kazakhstan, Kyrgyzstan, Tajikistan, Turkmenistan and Uzbekistan. The authorities' mechanisms of survey censorship vary across the region and the rules for survey companies are informal, fluid, human-dependent and partly negotiable, which makes the collection of public opinion data an even more uncertain venture. As such, opinion polling centres' and researchers' access to the field varies across the region.

To date, Kyrgyzstan and Kazakhstan are more accessible to scholars and survey companies than Tajikistan, Turkmenistan and Uzbekistan. To conduct opinion research in some Central Asian countries, opinion polling centres need to obtain an official letter from the respective authorities. The process of obtaining the necessary permission letters to conduct opinion research in Turkmenistan, Tajikistan and Uzbekistan is challenging and time-consuming. For that reason, my team and I use the help of our local partner organisations, who usually have to submit our detailed survey questionnaire to the respective authorities for pre-approval. Depending on the nature of the topic, questionnaires can be rejected. For example, amidst the border disputes between Tajikistan and Kyrgyzstan (Najibullah, 2023), Tajik authorities denied requests to conduct research in the border areas of the countries.

While in Tajikistan, survey companies usually have to obtain the necessary approval letter from the security services, in Uzbekistan, it can be any ministry from which they need to get the permission. Opinion polling centres are requested to obtain these permission letters for their local partner institutions that conduct the interviews in the respective *mahallas* (Uzbek word for "community"). The local interviewers then need to show this letter to each *mahalla* committee. Thus, while we have witnessed a boom in survey research under Mirziyoyev's reign, opinion polls that feature questions about politics and sensitive topics continue to be closely monitored by the Uzbek authorities (Dall'Agnola, 2023a). For example, it is hard for our contractors to conduct individual interviews, because sometimes, a representative of the *mahalla* committee may want to stand nearby to check if the interviewer is really asking the questions outlined in the permission letter. Under the watchful gaze of the representative of the *mahalla* committee, respondents often feel pressured to self-censor and answer questions in line with the Uzbek government's stance on a particular topic or issue. This phenomenon is also associated with self-censorship and "autocratic bias" (Tannenberg, 2022, 592) is very common among respondents in all five Central Asian countries. Central Asian people have little trust in survey providers, and most believe that the opinion polling centre is conducting the research on behalf of the local government. This can lead to high rates of systematic non-responses and/ or biased answers, resulting in poor data (Chia, 2014).

While Uzbekistan has somewhat softened its stance on opinion polling over the last five years, inquiries into public opinion in Turkmenistan are even more difficult for survey companies and foreign researchers. This is because it is almost impossible for them to enter the country, let alone to conduct opinion research (Dall'Agnola, 2023a). CAB conducts polls in Turkmenistan through a local partner organisation that needs to remain anonymous for safety and security reasons. The rules in obtaining permission letters in Turkmenistan are even more complicated and vague than in Uzbekistan or Tajikistan.

While opinion polling without official permission letters can lead to the closure of opinion research centres, Central Asian authorities are also known for retroactively interfering in the transfer and dissemination of survey data. For example, the Uzbek authorities are currently blocking the transfer of public opinion data that was collected by a local Uzbek polling centre for the World Value Survey Secretariat in Uzbekistan in 2022 (Dall'Agnola, 2023a). Furthermore, while in Kyrgyzstan and Kazakhstan, opinion polling centres may face fewer problems in data collection and transfer than in the other Central Asian countries, they face similar difficulties in terms of the dissemination of the polls' results. For example, in March 2022, CAB conducted a snap poll in Kyrgyzstan on public attitudes towards the war in Ukraine, with the intent to publish the data as soon as the data collection was finished. Out of fear of potential governmental sanctions against our organisation, we were only able to partly publish the poll in September 2022, when the data was no longer relevant. Having families and livelihoods in the region contributes to greater self-censorship among both local researchers and survey companies. I am convinced that it would have been much easier for CAB to freely disseminate the data if I and my team were not predominantly people who were born and live in Central Asia.

Finally, this does not mean that Central Asian regimes do not see the benefit in opinion polls. Some authorities even run opinion polls themselves. In Kazakhstan and Uzbekistan, for example, public opinion polls are frequently conducted by government-organised organisations such as Yuksalish in Uzbekistan or by governmental think tanks such as the Kazakh Institute of Strategic Studies for internal use in Kazakhstan. Kazakhstani authorities are also known for running snap polls before elections and referendums to legitimise the regime (Sorbello, 2023). Comparing the survey results between the government-affiliated and independent survey providers, we observe stark differences in the level of support for political parties. For instance, while both Paper Lab and CAB's opinion polls found that 20 per cent of Kazakhstan's population was planning to vote for the Amanat party (Sorbello, 2023), the Public Opinion Foundation, in their study for KTK, a TV channel, claimed that 60 per cent were planning to vote for the same party (Zakon.kz, 2023). In short, whether polls conducted by the local authorities really capture the pulse of the public remains highly questionable.

Both challenges outlined above do not only contribute to the self-censorship of survey companies and the networks they work with. They also influence the questions opinion polling centres can ask in the region, as the next section shows.

Asking Sensitive Questions in an Authoritarian Context

Even surveyors in democratic societies carefully assess the sensitivity of their questionnaires before commissioning the full survey (Tourangeau & Yan, 2007). In the Central Asian context, however, even questions that seem unproblematic at first can be censored by local authorities or contracted partner institutions at a later stage (Dall'Agnola, 2023a; Haerpfer & Kizilova, 2020). For example, CAB has encountered situations where interviewers were arrested and their tablets were confiscated by local authorities, even though they had only conducted surveys on English language learning preferences. In Tajikistan and Turkmenistan, opinion poll centres cannot ask questions regarding Islam, anything relating to the LGBTQ + community or issues (Dall'Agnola, 2023a), or domestic or international politics, leaving aside any questions regarding the president or other authorities. Moreover, although CAB has been able to conduct polls on respondents' preferences towards other Central Asian countries in Turkmenistan, it is impossible to ask the same question in Tajikistan. The rules with regard to which questions can be asked and which are off-limits in the region and within specific countries are fluid and constantly changing. For example, in Kazakhstan, CAB did not face any specific problems with regard to survey questions about domestic politics until the *Qantar* and Russia's war in Ukraine in 2022.

To conduct opinion polls on sensitive topics, CAB regularly consults with its local contracted partner institutions about national political events and the applicability of new survey questions in their respective countries. Depending on the country, CAB has to slightly rephrase new questions by making them less specific or placing them in another part of the questionnaire. The incorporation of a new question into the Central Asia Barometer Survey wave can thus take up to several weeks, even though the initial research question submitted to CAB was well-formulated. For example, in 2022, CAB was asked to include a question on people's attitudes towards CCTV cameras in public spaces. Several local vendors expressed concerns about the political sensitivity of this question. To guarantee a high-response rate, local contractors proposed using more specific and positive language and to limit the focus of the question to CCTV cameras' role in reducing crimes. However, this new question slightly distorted the original aim of the question, which was to capture public attitudes towards various types of CCTV cameras, including those that are used to control the wider public. Unsurprisingly, more than 90 per cent of respondents surveyed in the five Central Asian countries were in favour of CCTV cameras that are used to reduce crimes (Central Asia Barometer, 2022).

The positionality of the researcher and the research teams is another important factor that influences questionnaire development. For example, when coordinating CAB's surveys on Russia's war in Ukraine, we noticed that the very naming of the conflict was a reason for debate within our extended network of survey providers. Countries in Central Asia consume a vast amount of Russian propaganda, and for some of the team members, the right way to name the conflict was "Russia's special military operation in Ukraine", while others demanded the use of "Russia's attack on Ukraine". To remain as impartial as possible, CAB ended up using "the conflict between Russia and Ukraine", which seemed to be the most neutral term available at that moment. The use of the same wording in later surveys I coordinated in the Caucasus was rejected by our local partner organisations in Georgia and Armenia as it was deemed to bias the question and encourage respondents to provide an answer in favour of Russia's decision to attack Ukraine. One possible way to measure respondents' self-censorship and "social desirability bias" (Kalinin, 2016, 191) would be to run so-called "list experiments" (Frye et al., 2023, 213). "The premise of list experiments is that if a sensitive question is asked in indirect fashion, respondents may be more willing to offer a truthful response even when social norms encourage them to answer the question in a certain way" (Blair & Imai, 2012, 48). This method is currently being used by scholars (Frye et al., 2023) and opinion polling centres (Levada Centre, 2022) to capture Putin's popularity among the Russian public since the outbreak of the war. Researchers who plan to commission public opinion surveys on sensitive topics in Central Asia should consider this method.

A survey company's chosen mode of data collection can also influence respondents' self-censorship and social desirability biases and therefore, the quality of the collected data. Despite the fact that our interviewers are frequently monitored, verbally abused, and from time-to-time even arrested by local authorities and the police, until very recently, CAB surveys mainly relied on tablet-assisted personal interviews (TAPI hereafter). TAPI is a face-to-face data collection method in which the interviewer uses a tablet to record the answers given during the interview. Only when the COVID-19 pandemic hit the region did CAB start to use phone polls in its opinion research activities.

The switch to using technology for random sampling of telephone numbers in phone polls, which is a probability-based sampling method, happened only recently in the region. Now, quota or convenience sampling methods, which often lack the solid scientific and theoretical basis needed to make inferences about the entire target population, are less used by survey providers (Langer, 2018). Moreover, while we still have to get official permission letters from local authorities to run phone polls, they are usually administered via in-home stations or computer-assisted telephone interview studios that enhance interviewer safety and are less costly and less time-consuming. This having been said, telephone polls also have limitations: For example, interviewers are less likely to build trust with their interviewees who tend to be more suspicious of having their answers recorded via telephone than in a face-to-face interview.

Moreover, since asking respondents for their verbal or written consent often increases their suspicion and unwillingness to participate in a phone or in-person interview, some of the survey providers do not ask people for their consent, which is a clear breach of ethical standards. This is something a responsible researcher may want to discuss specifically with their survey provider. Central Asians' reluctance to give their consent for an interview, even with assurance by the interviewer that their statements will be treated anonymously, is a well-known issue (Dall'Agnola 2023b; Heathershaw & Mullojonov, 2020; Skriptaite, 2023) that ethics committees need to take into account when reviewing researchers' research proposals.

While there is a growing body of literature that highlights the advantages of online polls over telephone and in-person interviews in authoritarian contexts (Heerwegh, 2009), thus far, CAB has not used online polls to capture public opinion for two reasons: First, most online polls do not use probability-based sampling methods and therefore are not representative of the wider population (Langer, 2018). Second, since access to the Internet and social media still remains poor in Central Asia, especially in rural areas and among older generations (Dall'Agnola & Wood, 2022), online opinion polls mainly capture the views of urban youth.

Concluding Thoughts

As I have tried to show, it is important for the survey researcher to acknowledge and consider the diverse access barriers to the Central Asian field. Access to the different Central Asian countries varies and depends not only on the political and social developments in the respective country, but also on the researcher's positionality. Moreover, conducting opinion polls without permission letters from the local authorities in Tajikistan, Turkmenistan and Uzbekistan is sanctioned and can not only lead to the closure of local opinion research centres, but also to the arrest of the interviewers by the local police. The self-censorship bias in authoritarian contexts is an important issue to be considered by the researcher while working on their survey questionnaire, as is the dynamic list of sensitive questions pertinent to each country.

References

Asia Barometer. (2005). Surveys 2005. https://www.asianbarometer.org/survey/survey-timetable. Accessed December 20, 2022.
Blair, G., & Imai, K. (2012). Statistical analysis of list experiments. *Political Analysis, 20*(1), 47–77. https://doi.org/10.1093/pan/mpr048
CAB. (2023). Applied social research in Central Asia. Available here: https://ca-barometer.org/en. Last accessed April 25, 2023.
Central Asian Barometer Data. (2022). Kazakhstan, Kyrgyzstan, Tajikistan, Turkmenistan and Uzbekistan. Wave 12. Available at http://www.ca-barometer.org
Chia, S. (2014). How authoritarian social contexts inform individuals' opinion perception and expression. *International Journal of Public Opinion Research, 26*(3), 384–396. https://doi.org/10.1093/ijpor/edt033
CISR. (2023). The center for insights in survey research (CISR). Available here: https://www.iri.org/what-we-do/programs/cisr/. Last accessed April 25, 2023.
Dall'Agnola, J. (2023a). Smartphones and public support for LGBTQ+ in Central Asia. *Central Asian Survey.* https://doi.org/10.1080/02634937.2023.2187346
Dall'Agnola, J. (2023b). Fieldwork under surveillance: A research note. *Surveillance & Society, 21*(2).https://doi.org/10.24908/ss.v21i2.16455
Dall'Agnola, J., & Wood, C. (2022). Introduction: The mobilising potential of communication networks in Central Asia. *Central Asian Affairs, 9*(1), 1–15. https://doi.org/10.30965/22142290-12340013
Frye, T., & Gehlbach, S., Marquardt, K., & Reuter, O. (2023). Is putin's popularity (still) real? A cautionary not on using list experiments to measure popularity in authoritarian regimes. *Post-Soviet Affairs, 39*(3), 213–222. https://doi.org/10.1080/1060586X.2023.2187195
Haerpfer, C., & Kizilova, K. (2020). Values and transformation in Central Asia. In A. Mihr (Ed.), *Transformation and development* (pp. 7–28). Springer. https://doi.org/10.1007/978-3-030-42775-7_2
Heathershaw, J., & Mullojonov, P. (2020). The politics and ethics of fieldwork in post-conflict environments: The dilemmas of a vocational approach. In B. Bliesemann de Guevara & M. Bøås (Eds.), *Doing fieldwork in areas of international intervention: A guide to research in violent and closed contexts*, (pp. 93–112). Bristol University Press. https://doi.org/10.46692/9781529206913.007

Heerwegh, D. (2009). Mode differences between face-to-face and web surveys: An experimental investigation of data quality and social desirability effects. *International Journal of Public Opinion Research, 21*(1), 111–121. https://doi.org/10.1093/ijpor/edn054

Kalinin, K. (2016). The social desirability bias in autocrat's electoral ratings: Evidence from the 2012 Russian presidential elections. *Journal of Elections, Public Opinion and Parties, 26*(2), 191–211. https://doi.org/10.1080/17457289.2016.1150284

Langer, G. (2018). Probability versus non-probability methods. In D. Vannette & J. Krosnick (Eds.), *The Palgrave handbook of survey research* (pp. 351–362). Palgrave Macmillan.

Levada Centre. (2022). Doverie oprosam o spetsoperatsii. Available here: https://www.levada.ru/2022/11/01/doverie-oprosam-o-spetsoperatsii/. Last accessed May 5, 2023.

Najibullah, F. (2023, February 28). Kyrgyzstan And Tajikistan tout 'progress' on dangerous border dispute. Radio free Europe. https://www.rferl.org/a/kyrgyzstan-tajikistan-tout-progress-border-dispute/32292365.html

Skriptaite, R. (2023). The academic lion skin. balancing doctoral research with motherhood. In J. Dall'Agnola, A. Edwards, & M. Howlett (Eds.), *Researching in the former soviet union. stories from the field*. BASEES/Routledge Series. https://doi.org/10.4324/9781003144168-11

Sorbello, P. (2023, March 20). Limited choice and no transparency: Democracy kept at bay in Kazakhstan's elections. *Vlast.kz*. https://vlast.kz/english/54399-limited-choice-and-no-transparency-democracy-kept-at-bay-in-kazakhstans-elections.html

Tannenberg, M. (2022). The autocratic self-bias: Censorship of regime support. *Democratization, 29*(4), 591–610. https://doi.org/10.1080/13510347.2021.1981867

The Life in Kyrgyzstan Study. (2023). The 'life in Kyrgyzstan' study: A research-based, open access knowledge infrastructure for Central Asia. Available here: https://lifeinkyrgyzstan.org/. Last accessed April 25, 2023.

Tourangeau, R., & Yan, T. (2007). Sensitive questions in surveys. *Psychological Bulletin, 133*(5), 859–879. https://doi.org/10.1037/0033-2909.133.5.859

World Bank. (2023). Study "listening to the citizens of Uzbekistan." Available at: https://www.worldbank.org/en/country/uzbekistan/brief/l2cu. Last accessed April 25, 2023.

Zakon.kz. (2023b, March 11). 80.7% oproshennykh kazakhstantsev budut golosovat na vyborakh v mazhilis. *Zakon.kz*. https://www.zakon.kz/6386715-807-oproshennykh-kazakhstantsev-budut-golosovat-na-vyborakh-v-mazhilis.html

Kasiet Ysmanova is the Director at the Central Asia Barometer where she is responsible for the analytical design, collection and implementation of cross-national surveys in the five different Central Asian countries of Kazakhstan, Kyrgyzstan, Tajikistan, Turkmenistan and Uzbekistan. She has over three years of experience in carrying out public opinion polls all over Central Asia. She holds an MA in Politics and Security from the OSCE Academy in Bishkek, Kyrgyzstan.

Open Access This chapter is licensed under the terms of the Creative Commons Attribution 4.0 International License (http://creativecommons.org/licenses/by/4.0/), which permits use, sharing, adaptation, distribution and reproduction in any medium or format, as long as you give appropriate credit to the original author(s) and the source, provide a link to the Creative Commons license and indicate if changes were made.

The images or other third party material in this chapter are included in the chapter's Creative Commons license, unless indicated otherwise in a credit line to the material. If material is not included in the chapter's Creative Commons license and your intended use is not permitted by statutory regulation or exceeds the permitted use, you will need to obtain permission directly from the copyright holder.

Chapter 4
'Swiping Right'—The Ethics of Using Tinder as a Recruitment Tool in the Field

Paolo Sorbello

Abstract This article delves into the risks and pitfalls of using dating apps as participant recruitment tools in the field. To source people who worked in Kazakhstan's oil industry for my Ph.D. research in 2018, I made use of various popular social media apps such as Facebook and LinkedIn as well as the dating app Tinder. In an effort to "normalise" heterodox recruiting methods, in this essay, I seek to openly discuss how Tinder helped me recruit women working in the oil sector who, under less informal circumstances, would not have agreed to talk to me for my research.

Keywords Kazakhstan · Oil · Labour · Tinder · Fieldwork

Introduction

When I carried out fieldwork for my doctoral dissertation in Kazakhstan, I knew I had to navigate a half-familiar environment. I had spent a year in Almaty to complete a double-degree master's programme just four years earlier and had been following current affairs and maintained friendships and contacts in the country since then. Yet, my research scope had expanded geographically and narrowed disciplinarily, which meant that my existing contacts only represented, at best, a gateway to the sources I would need for the qualitative aspect of my research.

In Kazakhstan, I knew I would be facing obstacles typical of an authoritarian country. In the context of doing fieldwork, Menga linked the authoritarian setting with Bentham's panopticon, an "effective system of surveillance, based on the principle that power should be visible but also unverifiable" (Menga, 2020, 345. See also Hervouet, 2019, 95). Within the context of an authoritarian country, which roots its GDP growth in hydrocarbon exports, my research on labour, trade unions and precarity could be identified as a hostile topic by both oil companies and the authorities. In 2011, special forces shot at striking oil workers in the town square

P. Sorbello (✉)
Ca' Foscari University of Venice, Venezia, Italy
e-mail: paolo.sorbello@unive.it

© The Author(s) 2024
J. Dall'Agnola and A. Sharshenova (eds.), *Researching Central Asia*,
SpringerBriefs in Political Science,
https://doi.org/10.1007/978-3-031-39024-1_4

of Zhanaozen, killing at least 17. Oil enterprises, especially transnational companies (TNCs), often discourage trade union membership upon hiring their employees (Sorbello, 2021). Talking to workers in the oil sector, in certain contexts, could have put them at risk and could have created problems for me as well. Giulio Regeni, a former Ph.D. candidate at the University of Cambridge who was researching labour issues in Egypt was killed by the country's security services in January 2016, just months before I started my Ph.D. journey at the University of Glasgow and exactly two years before my fieldwork kicked off. Regeni's murder had prompted universities to be stricter, more focussed on reducing risks (Menga, 2020, 347). As such, the University of Glasgow emphasised the need for an air-tight ethics foundation for my own field research on labour issues in Kazakhstan.

My previous connections were the starting point for my research, the way I set in motion the so-called "snowball effect". Out of 115 interviews that contributed to my work (more on how I counted them below), 100 were the result of domino effects, with sources advising me to contact someone and giving me their number. Some were impromptu attempts to speak to someone at a conference or in a business centre. Several came through cold-contacting people on social media, mostly LinkedIn and Facebook (the expert and professional community I targeted was still using Facebook in 2018).

The following section of the article explores the ethical questions that arose from recruiting via social media platforms. In the third section, I address my experience of using Tinder as a recruiting tool for sources and how I navigated my positionality as well as mitigated ethical pitfalls in the process.

Social Media Recruiting and Ethics

The objective of lengthy academic ethics processes is to ensure that the universities are protected from any responsibility. At the University of Glasgow, the ethics board wanted me to establish clear paths to obtain consent and to ensure my own safety. The university also wanted me to take measures to establish clear communication with my sources and make sure they understood the purpose of our meetings. Aware of the risks, especially concerning local sources, I took the liberty of reversing the above-mentioned objectives: my foremost goal was to protect the people I spoke to, recognizing that complete protection is unattainable. Second, I worried about my own security; third, I worried about the university's reputation. I implemented this strategy when recruiting sources in person and online, a process that proved difficult despite my previous study experience in Kazakhstan.

Bureaucratic barriers and gatekeepers with little knowledge of the implications of academic research can represent an insurmountable obstacle to reaching certain individuals (e.g. HR managers at oil companies or trade union leaders) in the country. In an effort to establish trust, it was often better to contact interviewees via Facebook, Twitter and LinkedIn after having sent them a detailed email, which seldom reached their inboxes. The context of doing fieldwork is important and such barriers to recruitment were an issue that I had to raise with the University's ethics committee, which had no clear-cut guidelines on social media recruiting at the time.

Social media has become an increasingly important tool of recruitment for research due to the amount of information that public and private individuals voluntarily disclose on various platforms (Condie et al., 2018). Despite growing popularity among academics, according to Gelinas et al. (2017, 3) "there is no specific regulatory guidance and few resources to guide institutional review boards" and ethics committees. Importantly, on the other side of the coin, none of the social media apps that I used had regulations against the use of their platforms for research purposes.

These platforms are useful for building personal and professional networks with other users, even as the social media company sells advertisements and re-sells personal data for a profit (Zuboff, 2019). This—minus the personal data part—is essentially the same role that academic or industrial conferences play in the life of a researcher or a businessperson. Social networking whether for private or professional reason can happen during a coffee break or through the screen of a handheld device.

While scholarship on the ethics of using dating apps for networking is still scant, it remains true that "regardless of the country, culture, or social network, relationships can become sexualized" (Kovàcs & Bose, 2014, 116) between researchers and sources, something I tried to avoid. Subscribing to the methodological approach of "non exceptionalism" when using different recruitment methods (Gelinas et al., 2017, 5), I applied the same academic rigour to my use of every social media platform for research purposes.

After having attended a number of industrial and academic conferences prior and during my Ph.D. fieldwork, I noticed that most of the people I wanted to interview for my research had a social media profile on Facebook and, to a lesser extent, on LinkedIn and Twitter. As a result, I started to use Facebook as a participant recruitment tool, especially during my travels to Atyrau and Uralsk, two of the regions that I had not previously visited and where I lacked local contacts. Facebook groups of people working in the oil industry, expatriate workers (expats) and locals offering apartments for rent were a bountiful pool of potential interviewees given that my target sources were varied, ranging from company managers and senior bureaucrats to line workers and trade union leaders. Some contacts kindly pointed me to the Facebook or LinkedIn profiles of their colleagues and friends, or gave me their phone number, saying: "you can reach them via WhatsApp", yet another social media link. In Kazakhstan, it was and still is quite common to obtain the work or personal mobile number of senior managers or government workers, something that could be considered cross-over between professional and personal life in other countries. As Brasher (2020, 8) writes, "the control we have over the way our personal and professional identity as researchers is represented is much more in flux and subject to the rapidly changing technological landscape than it was just ten or twenty years ago". Using contacts obtained through social media and the sharing of personal information and contacts had the advantage of establishing an immediate and less austere link, but entailed the drawback of blurring the line between personal and professional spaces.

I only had one local phone number during my 10-month field trip to Kazakhstan. I still retained my UK phone number for my WhatsApp, which appeared to be a guarantee of legitimacy when I gave it to my contacts: "Oh, is this your Scottish number?" they would ask. Again, Brasher (2020, 11) argues that "researchers always bring with them into the field a multiplicity of identities that cleave along various and conflicting lines of power and privilege". In my case, I was sometimes assigned expert and authoritative status on my research topic and other times questioned or challenged as an outsider. Having only one smartphone with a working SIM card also meant that my personal and professional lives often intersected. Friends, family and relationships were in the same apps on my phone as my sources, an issue seldom talked about in academia. At some point, for personal reasons, I downloaded for the first time the Tinder application.

The Ethics and Practice of "Swiping Right"

My use of social media to gather source contacts had been successful in the first two months, during which time I was also—on a personal level—signed up to the dating app Tinder. Compared to other social media apps, Tinder was fairly new in 2018 in Kazakhstan when I used it for source recruitment. As a rather conservative dating environment (Dall'Agnola & Thibault, 2021), Kazakhstan had never experienced the presence of other dating apps or websites before, and the general approach to the Tinder app was one of "social discovery", rather than outright dating. The use of this app was not widespread in Kazakhstan. It was mostly used in Almaty, the city-headquarter for my fieldwork, and a little in Astana, the capital.

At the time, one could only sign up for Tinder by linking their Facebook profile, which I had done. The company managing the app used this authentication factor as a rudimentary attempt to avoid bots and to obtain basic personal data. The app, in fact, scraped the user's Facebook profile, including age, "likes", education and, crucially for my purposes, workplace and job position. At first, I leafed through the app trying to understand its spirit, discovering that Tinder users in Kazakhstan tried to find a wide range of connections, from life partners to one-night stands, from language buddies to company for a hike. I went on a few dates, saw theatre performances, improved my non-academic Russian and made new connections in Almaty, my first destination during my Ph.D. field trip.

The app geolocates your position, thus making it easier to see which other users are "nearby" which at most means within a 100-km radius. When, during my first month, I visited the Mangistau region to the west, I noticed that, among the few people who had uploaded their profile on the app, several displayed workplaces related to the oil sector. Working in the oil sector was and is still seen as an element of pride, this is perhaps why women chose to show it in their profiles. Tinder became useful in more remote locations such as Mangistau or Kyzylorda or Atyrau, where my original network was smaller. In addition, in these remote locations, it was more likely to find sources who worked in the oil sector because the local economy depended largely on extractive industry. Since the app displayed users' workplaces, I decided to then change my use of the app. I started trying to "match" with women working in the oil industry. In cases where they also "swiped right" on my profile, I was able to message them and explain the purpose of my desired meeting with them. In plain language, in English or Russian, I would describe at length my work in Kazakhstan, the nature of my research, and my need for an informal, anonymous conversation about the industry. Several app users that I "matched" with either did not respond to my request or declined the offer, possibly because an academic conversation over an afternoon tea was not what they were looking for while swiping profiles through Tinder, especially after having matched with me, a white male in his thirties.

My positionality could have played a deceptive role in the relationship that the use of the app created between me and my potential local sources. My public profile on Tinder did not openly disclose what I was looking for while using the app. Other users could not guess, just by leafing through my pictures, whether I was looking for a date or a language buddy. All that users could infer was that I was a 33-year-old white male, whose name was Paolo, and who spoke English, Russian, Italian and Spanish. In the application's settings, I chose to be visible only to women within a 100-km range of my geolocation. For some of the local women, meeting a foreign man is seen as a potential for social mobility, given that, particularly in resource-rich countries, foreign men, especially from the west, are usually richer than local men. Under these circumstances, according to previous research (Killick, 1995), the potential to start a relationship and eventually marry a foreign man could be another incentive for women to accept a meeting with a white heterosexual non-local male researcher. By being honest that I was not romantically available, I tried to navigate women's potential romantic expectations towards me.

My choice to only match with women on Tinder was intentional and mainly served to protect myself from physical harm, as widespread homophobia is still present in Kazakhstan (Dall'Agnola, 2020). Any hint that I was interested in meeting with another man could have attracted the unwanted attention of homophobic men who use the app to harass and out gay men (Dall'Agnola, 2023). Moreover, I had previously witnessed and reported incidents of hostility and aggression towards non-heterosexual men (Sorbello, 2014).

The choice to only look for women when using the Tinder app also helped me balance the gender makeup of the roster of my interviewees. Given that the oil sector is a male-dominated industry, finding women eager to share their views with me was a challenge, especially via traditional channels. Through Tinder, I found a dozen sources (out of more than 100 that I interviewed for my research), which only marginally helped with the gender balance, which was ultimately split 66:34 in favour of men. Tinder also allowed me to reach a wider range of job positions and seniority, something that would have hardly been possible during the traditional drop-in at an oil company or manpower agency due to the massive employment of women in secretarial or junior roles (Sorbello, 2023).

Aware of the ethical pitfalls of using a dating app for academic research (Condie et al., 2017), I went to great lengths to reduce risks and incomprehension for my sources once a woman working in the oil sector "matched" with me on Tinder by both explaining in writing and in person that the encounter would be of a strictly professional nature. To avoid any further misunderstandings, I also organised the meetings in public spaces, such as cafes, and during daylight hours. This was done in an effort to also minimise the potential feeling of threat or ambiguity. In fact, "meeting a respondent in a public place implies that neither they nor we are uncomfortable about being seen together. This fits with our general commitment to being open about what we do" (Glasius et al., 2018, 66).

While my transparency with regard to the nature of my research helped me gain the trust of some respondents, a number of women I met through Tinder initially considered me "odd", because I used the app outside of its socially understood end goal. Local women in Kazakhstan "swiping right" on the profile of an Italian man in his thirties did not expect to match with a Ph.D. researcher interested in an interview. Several women said they would only be interested in meeting "with the goal of establishing a long-term, serious relationship", while others just sent a message with the amount they expected to receive from me as a payment to spend the night with them. Navigating through useless interactions became easy once I chose to use Tinder only for source recruitment, turning down any interaction that would not lead to an interview or could be considered awkward. Once trust was established, the interviews followed the regular pattern, and were only occasionally followed by additional questions online. Only on one occasion, with the purpose of introducing me to a new contact, did I meet one of the interviewees recruited via the Tinder app a second time.

Conclusion

A sizable number of the people I reached out to during my fieldwork either refused to meet or did not respond to my message. Of the dozen people that I ended up meeting via Tinder in public cafes during the day, all contributed with either valuable insight or pointed me in the direction of their colleagues. All of them were associated with the corporate dimension of the oil sector, and were thus more accustomed to speaking professionally to foreigners. Around a dozen, or 10 per cent of the interviews for my Ph.D. research were conducted this way, and I was able to obtain another handful of interviews via a snowball effect from those.

I found that being transparent and open about the purpose of the meeting was a successful strategy to navigate my female respondents' expectations towards me in the field. My interviewees always knew that our meeting was strictly professional. I also went to great lengths to anonymise my sources, to avoid misunderstandings and to make sure that our conversation would not jeopardise their job status or, worse, their well-being. Because I dealt with quite sensitive topics that at times had sparked the interest of the security services in Kazakhstan—such as the Zhanaozen events of 2011, during which members of the foreign press were detained and several local journalists and human rights advocates were arrested (Rittmann, 2021)—I decided to leave no trace of my presence behind and to avoid pressuring people to meet. This meant that I had to forgo several potential interviewees. I am in no position to regret that, however, because I firmly abided by the principle of "do no harm", while still being conscious that "it can be hard to accept that your presence in the field may cause harm despite your best intentions as a researcher" (Brasher, 2020, 10).

As I have tried to show in this essay, the use of "unconventional apps", such as Tinder, for recruiting sources for research is a possibility that can and should be exploited in contexts where informal contacts are more customary. As I argue in my Ph.D. dissertation (Sorbello, 2021), the use of social media, messaging apps and social discovery apps should be openly embraced and used ethically and professionally, rather than dismissed because of a lack of specific regulation of these tools at the institutional ethics committee level. The limited ethical literature has been slow to catch up with the various methods of recruitment that researchers can employ in different contexts. In 2018, I found it useful to exploit the characteristics of the Tinder app for my research. While those could now be obsolete or of little use to other researchers, this essay aims to encourage a widening of the horizons of virtual recruiting tools, while maintaining ethical integrity.

References

Brasher, J. (2020). Positionality and participatory ethics in the global south: Critical Reflections on and lessons learned from fieldwork failure. *Journal of Cultural Geography, 37*(3), 296–310. https://doi.org/10.1080/08873631.2020.1760020
Condie, J., Lean, G., & Wilcockson, B. (2017). The trouble with tinder: The ethical complexities of researching location-aware social discovery apps. In K. Woodfield (Ed.), *The ethics of online research* (pp. 135–158). Emerald Publishing.
Condie, J., Lean, G., & James, D. (2018). Tinder matters: Swiping right to unlock research fields. In C. Costa and J. Condie (eds.), *Doing research in and on the digital: Research methods across fields of inquiry*. Routledge. https://doi.org/10.4324/9781315561622-7
Dall'Agnola, J. (2020). Queer culture and tolerance in Kazakhstan. In J. Dall'Agnola and J. Moradi (eds.), *PC on Earth. The beginnings of the totalitarian mindset* (pp. 99–116). Ibidem, Columbia University Press.
Dall'Agnola, J. (2023). Smartphones and Public support for LGBTQ+ in Central Asia. *Central Asian Survey*. https://doi.org/10.1080/02634937.2023.2187346
Dall'Agnola, J., & Thibault, H. (2021). Online temptations: Divorce and extramarital affairs in Kazakhstan. Religions 12, 654. https://doi.org/10.3390/rel12080654
Gelinas, L., Pierce, R., Winkler, S., Cohen, I., Fernandez, H., & Bierer, B. (2017). Using social media as a research recruitment tool: Ethical issues and recommendations. *American Journal of Bioethics, 17*(3), 3–14. https://doi.org/10.1080/15265161.2016.1276644
Glasius, M., de Lange, M., Bartman, J., Dalmasso, E., Lv, A., Del Sordi, A., Michaelsen, M., & Ruijgrok, K. (2018). *Research, ethics and risk in the authoritarian field*. Palgrave Macmillan.
Hervouet, R. (2019). A political ethnography of rural communities under an authoritarian regime: The case of Belarus. *Bulletin of Sociological Methodology/bulletin De Méthodologie Sociologique, 141*(1), 85–112. https://doi.org/10.1177/0759106318812790
Killick, A. (1995). The penetrating intellect: On being white, straight, and male in Korea. In D. Kulick & M. Willson (eds.), *Taboo. Sex, identity and erotic subjectivity in anthropological fieldwork* (pp. 76–106). Routledge.

Kovàcs, E., & Bose, A. (2014). Flirting with boundaries: ethical dilemmas of performing gender and sexuality in the field two tales from conservation-related field research in Hungary and India. In J. Lunn (ed.), *Fieldwork in the global south: ethical challenges and dilemmas*. Routledge. https://doi.org/10.4324/9780203096895

Menga, F. (2020). Researchers in the panopticon? Geographies of research, fieldwork, and authoritarianism. *Geographical Review, 110*(3), 341–357. https://doi.org/10.1080/00167428.2019.1684197

Rittmann, M. (2021, December 15). Workers' rights denied in Kazakhstan: Zhanaozen's legacy. *Human Rights Watch*. https://www.hrw.org/news/2021/12/15/workers-rights-denied-kazakhstan-zhanaozens-legacy

Sorbello, P. (2014, April 30). Homophobia Seethes in Kazakhstan. *The Conway Bulletin* (182). https://theconwaybulletin.com/blog/2014/04/30/homophobia-seethes-kazakhstan/ [permalink: https://bottleneckanalysis.files.wordpress.com/2023/04/homophobia-seethes-in-kazakhstan-the-conway-bulletin.pdf].

Sorbello, P. (2021). *Industrial relations in Kazakhstan's oil sector (1991–2019)*. PhD thesis, University of Glasgow. https://theses.gla.ac.uk/82271/

Sorbello, P. (2023). Hiring, firing, atomizing; Manpower agencies and precarious labour in Kazakhstan's Oil Sector. *International Labour and Working-Class History,* Forthcoming.

Zuboff, S. (2019). *The age of surveillance capitalism: The fight for a human future at the new frontier of power*. Public Affairs.

Paolo Sorbello holds a Ph.D. from the University of Glasgow. In his dissertation, he focused on labor relations in Kazakhstan's oil sector. He is a non-resident fellow at the Ca' Foscari University of Venice and a journalist living in Almaty. His academic works were published in *Central Asian Survey, Eurasiatica, Asia Maior*, and *The Routledge Handbook on Contemporary Central Asia*.

Open Access This chapter is licensed under the terms of the Creative Commons Attribution 4.0 International License (http://creativecommons.org/licenses/by/4.0/), which permits use, sharing, adaptation, distribution and reproduction in any medium or format, as long as you give appropriate credit to the original author(s) and the source, provide a link to the Creative Commons license and indicate if changes were made.

The images or other third party material in this chapter are included in the chapter's Creative Commons license, unless indicated otherwise in a credit line to the material. If material is not included in the chapter's Creative Commons license and your intended use is not permitted by statutory regulation or exceeds the permitted use, you will need to obtain permission directly from the copyright holder.

Part II
Beyond 'Outsiders' and 'Locals'

Chapter 5
The Power of a Multi-layered Identity in Central Asian Research

Gulzhanat Gafu

Abstract Conducting research in the Central Asian context is complex due to the competing historical, cultural, and linguistic narratives of the past(s) and present(s). In this essay, I, as a female Kazakh scholar, discuss how various aspects of my multi-layered positionality (e.g., gender, social status, motherhood, and institutional affiliation) shape my research in/on Central Asia. While critically reflecting on my insider versus outsider position, I also touch on my positionality as a single mother of three underaged children and how this influences the way I experience fieldwork.

Keywords Central Asia · Decoloniality · Local voice · Female scholar · Motherhood

Introduction

In recent decades, reflexivity as a methodological tool to acknowledge a researcher's positionality has become an important aspect of qualitative research, especially from critical, feminist, post-structural, and postmodern perspectives (Bilgen et al., 2021). Understanding one's positionality is crucial to recognize how it influences the research process, data collection, and interpretation of findings (Dall'Agnola, 2023). As noted by Chilisa (2012), failure to acknowledge and reflect on positionality can result in a biased or incomplete understanding of the research topic and its context.

Various publications have highlighted the difficulties associated with cultural differences when conducting research in non-western contexts, including Central Asia, especially when it comes to the dilemmas and challenges that are context specific (Jonbekova, 2020; Whitsel & Merrill, 2021). In communicating the challenges associated with doing fieldwork in the Central Asian context, much elaboration comes from international scholars. The issue of positionality is also distinct in the discourse of peers who come from outside.

G. Gafu (✉)
Nazarbayev University, Astana, Kazakhstan
e-mail: gulzhanat.gafu@nu.edu.kz

© The Author(s) 2024
J. Dall'Agnola and A. Sharshenova (eds.), *Researching Central Asia*,
SpringerBriefs in Political Science,
https://doi.org/10.1007/978-3-031-39024-1_5

In this essay, I reflect on my positionality as a female Kazakh scholar living and doing research in the context of Central Asia. Along with reflecting on my background and research experience as an early-career female researcher in the Central Asian context, I will follow decolonial thinking to question issues of power within my own positionality and representation as a local scholar. As argued by Bilgen et al. (2021, 520), "reflexivity in research processes can serve as a tool to dismantle embedded power hierarchies." My positionality is significantly influenced by my recent endeavors of questioning my own positionality as a western-educated local researcher from a traditional Kazakh family who was raised in a post-Soviet rural area in Kazakhstan. These constructs within my being clash with each other at times. While within the inner family, traditional views prevail, in my research practice, I am cautious of which values I am rooting into the knowledge I am producing. My traditionalism in thinking is also influenced by religious beliefs and culture in the family and larger society.

For that purpose, I first start with reflections on my Ph.D. journey in a UK university as a governmental scholarship holder, before continuing to discuss my postdoctoral experience at an international institution in Kazakhstan. After contemplating the issue of insider and outsider positionality in doing research in Central Asia, the essay ends with a reflection on another critical aspect of my positionality, namely, my identity as a single mother.

A Multi-layered Identity

My positionality as a social science researcher in the Central Asian context is embedded in my age, gender, language, social role, institutional affiliation, and religion. I found being aware of and navigating these multiple identities is crucial in the field. This awareness of the multiple layers of my identity did not occur straightforwardly to me. My journey began when I started my Ph.D., overwhelmed with the technical concerns of writing a thesis and engaging in only limited reflexive activity, to now as a postdoctoral researcher, where every piece written and read is accompanied by self-reflecting questions and analysis. My orientation toward reflexivity and positionality has largely been influenced by the latest project I am involved in, one which looks into co-creating culturally relevant social science research ethics in Central Asia.

Within the country context, I found that one explicit aspect of power in fieldwork is connected to my institutional affiliation. Once as a Bolashak scholarship holder while doing my doctoral field research and later as a postdoc at Nazarbayev University, I observed how both gatekeepers and participants would show respect toward me, accept and trust in me as a representative of an advanced education system. When coming from London to collect interview data, my role as a young researcher would be emphasized by gatekeepers as "international," with specific credit given to my Bolashak awardee status. Affiliation with Bolashak and Nazarbayev University is strongly guided by the policy discourse of benchmarking Western standards, which impacts the way representatives of these systems are perceived. This might be specific to the academic environment in Kazakhstan, where all my fieldwork happened.

I had an impression from unofficial conversations with respondents and gatekeepers in Kazakhstan that it is prestigious and a privilege to be affiliated with these systems. These "prestigious" systems are perceived as "difficult to access" and acquaintance with me was seen as an advantage. There were times when people would ask me how to get employed or access these entities. In these cases, being open and straightforward about my role and status as a researcher helped me to manage and navigate people's expectations of me. This can be tough at times, as research participants were expecting something back as a reward for their involvement in my research. Despite my prestigious affiliations, my access to people, who were predominantly "men in power," was not that straightforward.

Central Asian local researchers have extensively covered in their reflexive writings the challenges associated with accessing representatives in power. Janenova (2019) highlights raising concerns over various research problems such as gaining access to governmental officials, conducting interviews and focus groups, and important ethical and safety aspects of being in the position of a local researcher. My experience with governmental officials is related to gaining access to and being constrained or reluctant to speak up. In my experience as a Ph.D. student doing fieldwork in Kazakhstan, I was ignored and had interview requests rejected on many occasions by "people in power" as Thibault (2021, 4) puts it. I was sent away by the representatives of the Ministry of Education and Science who would agree to talk to me when I contacted them, and then at the agreed upon time would excuse themselves with a busy schedule or a "hectic day." After trying to gain access to the site for two months, I decided to send an official request as I knew that those sent via official channels could not be ignored and the Ministry would have to send me a reply, whether the reply they would send would be informative enough was another concern. But I hoped to at least get some response and planned to treat it as data, knowing that very often, you get a non-committal reply from officials.

In contrast, on another occasion, I observed how being affiliated with a Western institution helped ease access to participants, especially when participants were high-level officials. Once participants were given the credentials of the internationally recognized institution and foreign professor-level researcher whom I was assisting, they would talk to me and agree to spare their time for an interview.

On the same field trip for my doctoral research, I was concerned about the way official education policymakers whom I managed to meet would question the choice of the Kazakhstani education context and qualitative methodology for my doctoral research. According to them, as a Ph.D. student studying abroad on the Bolashak scholarship, I should have selected other contexts to learn "best practices" and then implemented them in Kazakhstan. Since quantitative methodology is a traditional research methodology established since the Soviet period, I appreciated that they were coming from their policymaker position and long-standing form of inquiry accepted in the local science system. But, as an enthusiastic young researcher who was motivated to explore local issues, I felt discouraged.

At the same time, as has been discussed by many local researchers (e.g., see Turlubekova, 2023), there were challenges that I faced in the field as a local researcher in contrast with foreign/international researchers, even those more junior. While age is another particular aspect of Central Asian culture, it is quite specifically experienced when intersected with gender. In some circumstances, my research abilities as a young female researcher were questioned or devalued. On one occasion, a male top manager, instead of answering my questions, challenged the validity of my questions: "Is this a question?" "What kind of question is this?" In that situation, I felt mistreated as a little, stupid girl who had no rights or enough competency to approach the person in power. Such experiences added more frustration and decreased my confidence as a Ph.D. student. For someone who is just paving her way in the competitive field of academia and for whom doing research was challenging at times, such an experience did not add any encouragement but affected my professional self-esteem. For some time, I had the uncomfortable feeling of hesitation to approach positional leaders. Now, I regret that I chose this group as my participants to the extent that, in my teaching, I tell my students to think carefully about who their participants are for their research.

Being an Insider and Outsider

Discussions on the insider/outsider stance have proven to be complex. Merriam et al. (2001, 1) state the fluidity of the boundaries of the two states, arguing for "the reconstruing of insider /outsider status in terms of one's positionality vis-à-vis race, class, gender, culture and other." Similarly, I often find myself feeling both an insider and an outsider, a so-called "in-betweener" (Milligan, 2016, 248) while conducting research in my country and the region.

The fluidity or at times, complexity, of my insider/outsider stance has been very distinctly expressed and shaped within the Central Asian Research Ethics (CARE)[1] project I have been part of for the two years since 2021. As part of this large research project, we, the research team, are being challenged by our established worldviews as researchers. While I came into the project with strong Eurocentric values on how to do research due to my educational background, over the course of the project I started questioning my own stance and axiology. Keeping in mind that Central Asian research is influenced by multi-layered colonialism, meaning Western academic colonialism and Russian imperialism (Chankseliani, 2017), I draw a lot from Linda Tuhiwai Smith's (2021, xiii) decolonization framework to "decolonize our minds, our discourses, our understandings, our practices, and our institutions" and to challenge myself as a researcher from Central Asia educated and working in a West-affiliated higher education institution. I also found Tuhiwai Smith's assertion that "decolonization… is about centering our concerns and world views and then

---

[1] For more details about the project, please consult the following website: https://m.facebook.com/CentralAsianResearchEthics/?wtsid=rdr_0bsJ9gCibA05kjGVG.

coming to know theory and research from our own perspective and for our own purposes" (2021, 43) was helpful in reflecting on the research practices that I learned from the Western education system but apply in the local context.

Within this project, where I interact with participants from the three Central Asian countries of Kazakhstan, Kyrgyzstan, and Uzbekistan, my insider/outsider stances are questioned and reflexed upon very often. This is transforming my thinking and the way I see my own research practice. In a sense, I observe and acknowledge that these dynamics and the complexity of insider/outsider positionality are powerful every time we, as a team, collectively make sense of the data. On the one hand, I am a Central Asian and I am an insider in comparison with my non-Central Asian colleagues. On the other hand, I am an outsider to Kyrgyzstan and Uzbekistan as I am not from there. For example, while initially, I would perceive the Central Asian region as homogeneous owing to the shared regional cultural background, over the course of qualitative interviews, I realized that all three countries are different despite their shared Soviet legacy.

The advantage of being an insider is that it is reported to provide relatively easy access to the field sites and people due to knowledge of how the system works on the ground and/or local networks and connections the researcher has. A common Kazakh language and cultural aspects are additional benefits that I found helpful in gaining access to research sites and people in Kazakhstan. I was surprised by the openness and trust of the university administration and faculty members who I interviewed for my research. Due to the overwhelming political context and support for the phenomenon I studied, I expected that respondents might choose to be rather constrained in talking openly. But to my surprise, while cautious at the beginning, during the course of the interviews, more and more open and critical comments were explicitly shared with me. I believe one very decisive factor of such experience is grounded in the importance of acknowledging and respecting the "insider" relationship between myself and my research participants.

As a novice researcher engaged in my very first fieldwork, I was convinced of the privilege of my "insiderness." I found that this stance is amplified when intersected by language and ethnicity. For example, in the regions where people are predominantly Kazakh speakers, I was accepted as "one of us," who can understand by default the reality that underlies their responses. However, such ease comes with its own pressures as this insiderness subjugates objectivity and creates bias and needless assumptions instead of further probing to clarify what meaning the respondents place on their responses. For example, as a local researcher, oftentimes, I find myself not noticing or perhaps undermining some practices that are embedded within the culture that I grew up in and which feel "normal." However, my Western education background and interaction with international scholars in my academic career influence my thinking and I see how my positionality changes, and I question such issues as unethical. As a local, I understand the practices that are common, but from a Western perspective, they might be considered an issue creating a conflict inside.

For instance, writings of international female scholars who do fieldwork in Central Asia often highlight ethical dilemmas specific to the region that they found challenging to deal with due to the lack of cultural and contextual experience. Being an insider, in contrast, is helpful in navigating such ethical issues in the field. On the other side of the coin, as a local to the culture, you may overlook or ignore these issues. For example, Thibault (2021), as an outsider female researcher, discusses the tension of unwanted attention from Central Asian males while doing fieldwork in Tajikistan. In her fieldwork notes, she talks about frequent questioning of her marital status. Indeed, as discussed by foreign female scholars in the Central Asian context, being married and having kids is often welcomed by the wider Central Asian society (Peshkova, 2014; Skriptaite, 2023). Once Central Asians know your marital status, you are kind of "approved." From my own local experience, such questioning seems to be directed particularly at females, though male researchers might also get questions about their relationship status.

On Single Motherhood and Academia

As a single mother scholar, the boundaries between my roles as a parent and academic are often blurred (CohenMiller & Izekenova, 2022). The challenges of being an involved and present mother while also trying to catch up professionally as an emerging scholar in a competitive academic field can be daunting. These challenges can sometimes be further complicated by the cultural context in Central Asia encountered while conducting fieldwork. As a single mother, this can be especially challenging, as I must balance the demands of my research with the needs of my children. In the Central Asian context, with its strong emphasis on family values, being a single mother can be seen as a departure from traditional family structures and may be met with scepticism or disapproval by some members of the community. This scepticism can make it even more challenging to balance the demands of family and research, as there may be additional expectations and obligations placed on me as a mother. This can be particularly demanding while doing fieldwork which requires me to be away from home and my children for long periods of time.

When conducting one of my projects during COVID-19, and later when Zoom became part of our lives, like other mothers before me (Skriptaite, 2023), one of the challenges I experienced was from my underage children who, from time-to-time, would interrupt me with their different needs while conducting online recorded interviews. On several occasions, my children broke into the room with screams and cries to ask for water or for me to change their nappies. It was often funny to find out during the data analysis of the official interview transcripts, which were done by a third-party text, which read "The kid screams and asks to change her nappy." Though the majority of respondents were understanding, male participants, in particular, would be bothered by these occasional disruptions. Female respondents, in contrast, would be supportive and comment that they were also in the same boat. At times, as a researcher, I would be concerned about being perceived as unprofessional by my participants as deep in my mind, I find myself influenced by gendered stereotypes and mother role prejudices. As Skriptaite (2023, 139) writes, "these moments of 'exposure' and the inability to control" and separate my private and professional spaces "would make me feel like an imposter—a woman not fully in control of the domain traditionally assigned to her, who is miserably failing at posing as a professional—in a domain which by tradition is normally gifted to males."

Despite these challenges, I have learned to be resilient, creative, and reflective in my work. The strong family values traditionally emphasized in Kazakh culture have proven to be an invaluable resource for me as a researcher since I received immense support from my parents and relatives who have always been ready to take care of my kids whenever I needed to either travel to the field or conduct interviews in person. I am especially thankful for the tremendous and encouraging support and help that I, as a widowed single parent, received from my extended Kazakh family, friends, colleagues, and community. Such support is rewarding and keeps me committed to my academic journey.

Concluding Thoughts

The multi-layered nature of positionality, as discussed in this essay, is a complicated matter. Its complexity is underlined by various factors and is often context-bound. It is often more difficult to navigate when you are an emerging scholar from a region where research is seen as "under-developed," which puts extra pressure and tension on paving your way through to your research career. Being aware of your role and position in building knowledge in your own context with its nuances is an important part of the whole research process.

Being reflective has helped me to appreciate my position as a local researcher, which in turn can be helpful in developing a deep understanding of the nuances of the problem and its context, in building strong relationships with community members and stakeholders, in providing access to valuable insights and perspectives, and in opening opportunities for collaboration and co-creation. At the same time, I also acknowledge the potential for bias or a lack of objectivity, as researchers may be personally invested in the issues they are studying. It is important for local researchers to remain vigilant and transparent about their biases, and to ensure that their research is rigorous and methodologically sound.

Reflecting on my experiences as a single mother and scholar conducting fieldwork, I have come to appreciate the resilience and adaptability that this work requires. By being creative, strategic, and reflective in my approach, I have been able to navigate the competing demands of family and research, while also building a fulfilling and meaningful career, albeit one which requires careful planning and prioritization. By setting boundaries, delegating tasks when possible, and being intentional about how I use my time, I am able to be both an involved mother and a successful academic. While it is not always easy, I am grateful for the opportunities and experiences that come with balancing these two roles, and I hope to continue to grow and learn in both my personal and professional life.

References

Bilgen, A., Nasir, A., & Schöneberg, A. (2021). Why positionalities matter: Reflections on power, hierarchy, and knowledges in 'development' research. *Canadian Journal of Development Studies/revue Canadienne D'études Du Développement, 42*(4), 519–536. https://doi.org/10.1080/02255189.2021.1871593

Chankseliani, M. (2017). Charting the development of knowledge on Soviet and post-Soviet education through the pages of comparative and international education journals. *Comparative Education, 53*(2), 265–283. https://doi.org/10.1080/03050068.2017.1293407

Chilisa, B. (2012). *Indigenous research methodologies.* SAGE Publications.

CohenMiller, A., & Izekenova, Z. (2022). Motherhood in academia during the COVID-19 pandemic: An international online photovoice study addressing issues of equity and inclusion in higher education. *Innovative Higher Education, 47*(5), 813–835. https://doi.org/10.1007/s10755-022-09605-w

Dall'Agnola, J. (2023). The challenges of fieldwork in Post-Soviet Societies. In J. Dall'Agnola, A. Edwards, & M. Howlett (eds.), *Researching in the former Soviet Union.* BASEES/Routledge Series. https://doi.org/10.4324/9781003144168-1

Janenova, S. (2019). The boundaries of research in an authoritarian state. *International Journal of Qualitative Methods, 18*, 1–8. https://doi.org/10.1177/1609406919876469

Jonbekova, D. (2020). Educational research in Central Asia: Methodological and ethical dilemmas in Kazakhstan, Kyrgyzstan and Tajikistan. *Compare: A Journal of Comparative and International Education, 50*(3), 352–370. https://doi.org/10.1080/03057925.2018.1511371

Merriam, S., Johnson-Bailey, J., Yeh-Lee, M., Kee, Y., Ntseane, G., & Muhamad, M. (2001). Power and positionality: Negotiating insider/outsider status within and across cultures. *International Journal of Lifelong Education, 20*(5), 405–416. https://doi.org/10.1080/02601370120490

Milligan, L. (2016). Insider-outsider-inbetweener? Researcher positioning, participative methods and cross-cultural educational research. *Compare: A Journal of Comparative and International Education,* 46 (2), 235–250. https://doi.org/10.1080/03057925.2014.928510

Peshkova, S. (2014). *Women, islam, and identity: Public life in private spaces in Uzbekistan.* Syracuse University Press.

Skriptaite, R. (2023). The academic lion skin. Balancing Doctoral research with motherhood. In J. Dall'Agnola, A. Edwards, & M. Howlett (eds.), *Researching in the former Soviet Union. Stories from the Field.* BASEES/Routledge Series. https://doi.org/10.4324/9781003144168-11

Thibault, H. (2021). 'Are you married?': Gender and faith in political ethnographic research. *Journal of Contemporary Ethnography, 50*(3), 395–416. https://doi.org/10.1177/0891241620986852

Tuhiwai, S. (2021). *Decolonizing methodologies: Research and indigenous peoples.* Zed Books.

Turlubekova, Z. (2023). A woman of her word prepared for the worst: Researching drug trafficking in Kazakhstan. In J. Dall'Agnola, A. Edwards, & M. Howlett (eds.), *Researching in the former Soviet Union. Stories from the field.* BASEES/Routledge Series. https://doi.org/10.4324/9781003144168-11

Whitsel, M., & Merrill, M. (2021). Towards building a culturally informed consent process in Central Asia. *Central Asian Survey, 40*(3), 351–367. https://doi.org/10.1080/02634937.2021.1898338

Gulzhanat Gafu is a postdoctoral scholar at the Nazarbayev University Graduate School of Education. She holds a Ph.D. degree in Comparative and International Higher Education from the University College London's Institute of Education. Her research interests are internationalisation of higher education and research ethics, sustainable education and graduate skills and competencies. Currently, she is working on an independent research grant on sustainable education in Kazakh universities. In the past, she has taught graduate students at various universities and held various senior positions in different higher education agencies in Kazakhstan.

Open Access This chapter is licensed under the terms of the Creative Commons Attribution 4.0 International License (http://creativecommons.org/licenses/by/4.0/), which permits use, sharing, adaptation, distribution and reproduction in any medium or format, as long as you give appropriate credit to the original author(s) and the source, provide a link to the Creative Commons license and indicate if changes were made.

The images or other third party material in this chapter are included in the chapter's Creative Commons license, unless indicated otherwise in a credit line to the material. If material is not included in the chapter's Creative Commons license and your intended use is not permitted by statutory regulation or exceeds the permitted use, you will need to obtain permission directly from the copyright holder.

Chapter 6
Being Afghani, French and not Soviet Along the Border Between Tajikistan and Afghanistan

Mélanie Sadozaï◉

Abstract How can being a French woman of Afghan origin be an asset and an obstacle in conducting research along the borderlands of Badakhshan between Tajikistan and Afghanistan? This essay draws on field anecdotes which fostered critical thinking about my positionality as a French-Afghani woman. While my French passport symbolized my foreign identity, having personal ties with Badakhshan made me not "just a foreigner" due to my Afghan heritage. I argue that having a plural identity is just as helpful in conducting ethnographic research as it can be difficult to maintain the necessary distance from the object of study and to keep my collaborators safe.

Keywords Border · Foreigner · Local · Danger · Family ties · Fieldwork

Introduction

Far from simply a research tool, fieldwork involves not only a displacement, a mode of investigation, but also a social relationship (Allès et al., 2016). The expression "doing fieldwork" is synonymous with trying to reduce, if not abolish, distances, whether they be metric, cultural, linguistic, or cognitive in order to create a "direct contact" between the researcher, their field, and the object of study (Steck, 2012, 77). This triangulation inevitably raises the issue of how the researcher's position influences the field process and the knowledge production thereof.

Located at the margins of the former Soviet space, the border between Tajikistan and Afghanistan, marked by the Pyanj River, lies at the core of my academic research. The cross-border region of Badakhshan and the interactions between Tajikistanis and Afghanis taking place there was my primary focus and my personal relation to the region made the question of positionality crucial for my research.

M. Sadozaï (✉)
The George Washington University, Washington, DC, USA
e-mail: melanie.sadozai@inalco.fr

INALCO/Sorbonne Paris Cité, Paris, France

© The Author(s) 2024
J. Dall'Agnola and A. Sharshenova (eds.), *Researching Central Asia*,
SpringerBriefs in Political Science,
https://doi.org/10.1007/978-3-031-39024-1_6

My interest in this border stemmed from my Afghan origins and personal background. My father had escaped Afghanistan the day before the Soviet troops entered Kabul in 1979 and had started a new life in France where he married my mother, a French woman of Breton heritage. Just like millions of Afghans (Sadozaï, 2021a), the war in Afghanistan had wrecked my father's ambition to live and work in his native country. In 2014, when I first traveled to the border between Tajikistan and Afghanistan, I was struck by the symbolic aspect of the Pyanj River: It was along this waterway that war "ended." Four years later, I decided to challenge this thought theoretically, drawing on my academic education in International Relations. I wanted to engage in a PhD project in which I could use my personal affinity to this border, as well as my local heritage.

Since the beginning of my research, I have understood that ethnographic methodology undertaken in these particular borderlands would necessitate reflective analysis and positionality in order for me to create the necessary distance from the object of study while being immersed in my research (Groulx, 1999). The matter of positionality has been tackled through the question *how* we are perceived, but not so much by *who* perceives us. I argue that my French-Afghani identity surely influenced the way I was seen in the field, but that it also depended highly on the categories of interlocutors I was dealing with.

Conducting fieldwork along a border with a country that has seen decades of war is highly symbolic. Along the border with Afghanistan, danger is often based on stereotypes, validating official narratives considering this border as a place subject to violence and drug trafficking (Sadozaï, 2021b). Like Sluka (1990, 124), I consider that the dangers are often exaggerated, based on stereotypes, media images, or inadequate information, and that "in most cases they are not insurmountable—as long as one takes them seriously and approaches them as an essential methodological concern." Questioning the notion of danger associated with the Northern border of Afghanistan, I show that, during my field trips, I faced "methodological risks" pertaining to my position as both a foreigner and a perceived local more than dangers to my own security.

This chapter draws on my stories of researching the border between Tajikistan and Afghanistan in Badakhshan between 2014 and 2022. First, I highlight how my French citizenship labeled me as a foreigner for the Tajikistani authorities. Then, I show how my Afghan heritage gave me unique access to this border and its borderland communities. Finally, I explore the emotional bias I faced and the strategy I found to overcome it.

The Foreign Passport as an Identity Marker

In Tajikistan, accessing the Afghan border requires overcoming administrative obstacles which are difficult to bypass for foreign passport holders, who must secure the special permit for the Autonomous Mountainous Province of Badakhshan—in Tajik, Viloīati Mukhtori Kūhistoni Badakhshon (VMKB)—along which runs more than half of the border with Afghanistan. The issuance of this document is not guaranteed: as foreigners, we have to cope with arbitrary decisions made by the local authorities, which represent important constraints to conducting fieldwork there. The border between Tajikistan and Afghanistan is even more unique as, during the Soviet times, it was highly monitored and was subject to a specific border regime. Thus, the perception of the border as unsafe, stemming from more than seventy years of suspicion toward Afghanistan, remains entrenched today in the minds of the Tajikistani authorities.

In this context, any stranger going to the Afghan border may be interrogated. On several occasions, I was stopped by police officers in Ishkashim outside of the official checkpoints. When I asked about the purpose of these identity checks, I was told, "We are at the Afghan border," without further explanation. These interactions were always cordial, certainly because I was often accompanied by locals from Ishkashim who inspired a form of trust for the local police. My friends who lived there explained to me that the police had to register the foreigners at the police station, but that it was also "routine" because the agents were terribly bored. The border with Afghanistan, in association with my French passport, was a pretext to break away from boredom and to perform authority.

The border is also a place where illegal practices take place, often conducted by those who are supposed to prevent them (De Danieli, 2011). Researchers and foreigners, in this particular border environment, can be categorized as belonging to one political movement or another, or be identified by the national intelligence services. In other cases, they may serve as a conduit to promote demands, make claims, or convey certain ideas abroad (Manos, 2010). For the border authorities, it was clear I was not from Tajikistan, and therefore my presence was suspicious, while anywhere else in Tajikistan, the police did not even pay attention to me.

In 2022, when traversing the border between Uzbekistan and Tajikistan by train with a friend who held a Russian passport at the time, my origins and gender revealed a very clear perception of "non-Soviet" people by the Tajikistani border control officer who had the power to give or deny us access to Tajikistan. To avoid any uncomfortable conversation that we may have faced, we pretended to be married. The officer argued that we had entered Tajikistan without filling out what he called a "mandatory" form. The only way out was for us to either go back to the border crossing point near Buston—a six-hour drive from Dushanbe—where we had our passports stamped or to "decide" and "suggest a solution" (in Tajik: *vaĭ kardan*; in Russian: *vybiraĭte/predlagaĭte*). As the officer answered a phone call, we understood that we had to "decide" to bribe him. I handed out a 20-euro bill. "*Malo!*" he yelled in Russian, "it's not enough!" My "husband" then explained that it was all we had. "I don't expect you to pay," the officer told him in Russian, thinking I would not understand. "You are Russian, you are from the former Soviet Union, like me. But your wife, she is French. She has to pay." Even when my "husband" replied that being married to him meant I was also Russian, the officer did not take it as an answer. After more bargaining, he eventually left with the 20 euros. I refused to shake his hand when he offered. He insisted in Tajik: "the doors of Tajikistan will always be open to you!".

In these two instances, the risk lay in the arbitrary decisions authorities along the borders could make regarding my presence in the country due to my foreign passport. This type of risk has been clearly identified in the literature on field research in former Soviet countries where suspicion towards foreigners is tied to authoritarianism (Hervouet, 2019).

Authoritarianism raises another important risk pertaining to our collaborators' safety. As outlined by Thibault (2023), many scholars researching in former Soviet countries have faced situations of being denied a visa, deportation, or becoming persona non grata. While Tajikistan has developed a more welcoming policy for foreign tourists, namely, by implementing a visa-free policy for 52 countries in January 2022, tension has grown toward foreigners since protests took place in VMKB in November 2021. Cases of Tajikistani citizens being imprisoned because of their suspected relations with foreigners have become a reality, as shown by the example of Ulfatkhonim Mamadshoeva (Sultanalieva, 2022). In a state-led television broadcast, this human rights activist was accused of fomenting riots in VMKB after receiving funding and instructions from an unnamed "Western" embassy (in Tajik: *gharbī*).[1] It is important to underline that our positionality as foreigners can not only prevent us from accessing the field, but more importantly, put locals, who do not hold a foreign passport, in high danger. In authoritarian regimes like Tajikistan, positionality does not only refer to *our* position, but to how our position as a foreigner can have a negative impact on our interlocutors. Ethical issues and protection of collaborators, as underlined by Shih (2015), must prevail over research goals. However, in the eyes of Tajikistani citizens in Badakhshan, my French passport never mattered; I was rather seen through my ancestral roots from the region.

Not 'Just a Foreigner'

A type of danger that I often hear of when talking about my fieldwork is that of being a lone woman. While I acknowledge that this is not true for all ethnographers of Central Asia (Dall'Agnola *in this volume*; Thibault, 2021), and even if I encountered uncomfortable situations—like a polite marriage proposal with a man thirty years older than me—my gender never hindered my research. I often argue that the reason is that I have never been alone in the field. I purposely traveled in shared vehicles, knowing that it would be the only way to observe and practice mobility along the border, while trusting my drivers. I would stay with families where sometimes three generations were living under the same roof. Because of this immersion, I always knew I had someone to rely on should any problem arise. Additionally, my personal perception of the field in Badakhshan was that of a peaceful place for foreign women.

This feeling of security also pertains to the fact that, in Badakhshan, I would sometimes pass as being *pomiri*, the term used to refer to the Ismaili inhabitants of VMKB in Tajikistan, and as an "Afghan" for Afghans. Afghans would hear me

---

[1] See the video on Youtube at https://www.youtube.com/watch?v=ZmPwdqoa1Mc.

speak Dari, and Tajikistanis knew I did not speak standard Tajik and assumed I had a Pamiri accent. "Are you Pamiri?" I was asked on many occasions. I would answer in Shughni, one of the Pamiri languages, but my command of it being limited, I would then admit to being French and Afghani. While some people believed me, others thought I was trying to hide that I was Pamiri. "You look like you are Pamiri" was then the argument they would hold on to. In fact, my father, whose own father was Pashtun, always knew he had relatives from the region of Sheghnan in Afghanistan on his mother's side. My grandmother's ancestors had traveled all over the region, from Badakhshan, to Kashmir and then Kabul. However, my father only recalled visits from his Sheghnan relatives in Kabul as a young boy in the 1960s and never got to trace back his lineage.

The identity of the researcher is valued differently by the individuals to whom they present themselves and depends on the situation they are in. They may be seen as outsider or insider, but also as "inbetweener," a notion which goes against the dichotomy of being either outside or inside and focuses rather on shifted positions (Milligan, 2016, 248). In her doctoral dissertation, Remtilla provides insights on her own shifted position from her fieldwork in Ishkashim, Tajikistan. Remtilla (2012, 28), an Ismaili woman from Canada, found that mentioning her religion to drivers or in the markets made her "an Ismaili sister" and no longer "just a foreigner." Akin to Remtilla's experience, referring to my origins from the region triggered sympathy from my Pamiri interlocutors. They often referred to me as *"Dukhtari Sheghnan"* (Dari/Tajik for "the daughter of Sheghnan"), in reference to a famous Afghan song praising the Sheghnani roots of a young girl. My family's ancestral ties to the region, even if obscure, marked me out as local, despite my French citizenship. For my interlocutors, it represented a legitimate reason to go back to what they considered my ancestral homeland in search of my roots in Badakhshan. This shifted my position from foreigner to a local in the eyes of the actual locals and made me, to quote Remtilla (2012, 28), not "just a foreigner."

Sharing ancestral ties and familiarity with the field facilitated my access to and interactions with people. While I presented myself as French, I did not hide that my father was born and raised in Afghanistan. On the other hand, I was careful not to reveal it until after the interviews to avoid influencing the answers and encouraging self-censorship. My background also allowed me to interact with the Afghans I met along the border, especially in cross-border markets, and gave me the opportunity to be easily integrated into the Afghan circles. Akin to the experience of Osman (2020, 9), who describes the perception of her Afghan origins by her interlocutors during her fieldwork in Afghanistan, the questions I was asked about my parents, a binational couple and therefore a "mixed" couple (in Tajik and Dari: *omekhta, aralash*), were mostly out of curiosity or a way of starting an exchange.

In Badakhshan, I explained that my paternal family had relatives who probably still lived in Sheghnan, Afghanistan, although this connection was unclear to us. It was assumed that these personal ties to the territory, although vague, explained my interest in the region. My host families, or even the people I briefly spoke to, were content with this brief introduction because they felt they knew enough about me. Additionally, after a few visits in the region, when asked where I had traveled in the Pamirs, I would list the different places I had traveled to, sometimes the precise villages, and would receive positive reactions. Just like in other understudied former Soviet places, interest for the people and the region we are visiting abolishes social distance and creates familiarity with the field (Hervouet, 2019). At the same time, it triggers emotions which can prevent us from reaching a form of objectivity.

Emotional Bias and "Empathic Neutrality"

Being seen as "not just a foreigner" resulted in both a risk of emotional bias and an opportunity for reflection on the topic. One of the questions I explored in my research pertained to Tajikistanis' perceptions of the border with Afghanistan. My own understanding of cross-border dynamics could have been biased by my Afghan origins and the proximity I felt with Afghans. It was crucial not to let my personal trajectory create this emotional bias. Establishing distance between the content of the responses regarding the perceptions of Afghans and my own perception of a group with whom I share common origins was necessary to prevent the analysis from being tainted by emotions.

Adopting an ethnographic method in a field that is not completely removed from the researcher's personal background involves asking questions of emotions, more particularly of empathy for the subjects. Paillé and Mucchielli (2016, 148) define empathy as an "alterocentric sensitivity, social sensitivity, receptivity to others' reactions." From a methodological perspective, the researcher's subjectivity forces them to carry out reflexive work in order to distance themselves from their object of study and their fieldwork, while at the same time being immersed in the research. I considered this emotional aspect of my research as a challenge to neutrality, while seeing it also as a way to engage in reflexivity. Like many researchers before me (Holmes, 2013; Patton, 1990; Thajib et al., 2019), I considered empathy as a descriptive method that allows me to relive the thoughts and experiences of local protagonists.

In their seminal work on grounded research, Glaser and Strauss (1967, 226) offer a strategy by calling for an "informed detachment." This method consists of finding the right balance between the necessary distance from the field and the subjects, and an indispensable proximity with them, so as not to neglect either of the two. Along with a number of qualitative methodologists, I have used this dual approach. Patton (1990, 111) has conceptualized it under the expression of "empathic neutrality," a notion which "offers a middle ground between becoming too involved, which can cloud judgment, and remaining too distant, which can reduce understanding." This method allowed me to engage with my own position as a French woman of Afghan heritage, perceived as a somewhat local, in order to avoid the emotional bias mentioned previously. For example, I was not aiming to have my Tajikistani respondents share positive opinions about Afghans just because of my Afghan heritage. I would frame the question in a way which gave them enough latitude to elaborate on any perception they held, whether negative or positive. Being neutral meant that I had "no axe to grind, no theory to prove (to test but not to prove), and no predetermined results to support" (Patton, 1990, 113), while being empathetic meant combining "cognitive understanding with affective connection" (Patton, 1990, 114).

Drawing on my own fieldwork experience, I encourage other scholars of local origins to apply Patton's concept of "empathic neutrality" to avoid falling into an excess of empathy for their respondents. The constant effort to be detached permitted me to integrate all types of perceptions shared by my respondents, to enrich my analysis of them, and to come to the conclusion that my initial assumption—that Afghans are negatively perceived by people in Tajikistan—is not necessarily true, and that the reality is more nuanced.

Conclusion

My academic research has surely been influenced by both my Afghan background and my French citizenship. Empirical scholars who have personal ties with their field can be biased, too compassionate, and lack objectivity in their analysis. Additionally, being French also proved that I was not seen as a local, particularly by border authorities in Tajikistan, as I lacked a Soviet identity. Positionality was thus a matter of being either a foreigner, or not "just a foreigner" who expressed empathy for her respondents.

At an early stage of my research, I sought to make the most of having local roots and a particular attachment to the field, while questioning the methodological considerations that this would imply. The emotional component of ethnographic research entails a risk of providing limited results. Rather than an obstacle, my proximity to the field due to my local origins proved to be an asset, turning difficulty into opportunity.

It is my hope that this chapter will be useful to early-career researchers and students considering fieldwork research in similar contexts, whether they are native to a place, have local origins, or no connection at all. It is important to underline that the comments and anecdotes I shared here should not serve as a general guideline for field research. Instead, I hope that my field experiences will encourage other scholars to reflect on their own positionality when interacting with their interviewees, collaborators, participants, or interlocutors in the field. More broadly, my reflections should serve as a reminder for us that we as scholars should always question the notion of danger to avoid causing harm in the field.

References

Allès, D., Guilbaud, A., & Lagrange, D. (2016). L'entretien En Relations Internationales. In G. Devin (Ed.), *Méthodes de Recherche En Relations Internationales* (pp. 159–176). Presses de Sciences Po.

Dall'Agnola, J. (2023). Introduction: The challenges of fieldwork in post-soviet societies. In J. Dall'Agnola, A. Edwards, & M. Howlett (Eds.), *Researching in the Former Soviet Union: Stories from the field* (pp. 1–16). Routledge.

Danieli, F. D. (2011). Counter-Narcotics Policies in Tajikistan and their impact on state building. *Central Asian Survey, 30*(1), 129–145. https://doi.org/10.1080/02634937.2011.554067

Glaser, B. G., & Strauss, A. L. (1967). *The discovery of grounded theory: Strategies for qualitative research.* Aldine Publishing Company.

Groulx, L. (1999). Le Pluralisme En Recherche Qualitative: Essai de Typologie. *Revue Suisse De Sociologie, 25*(2), 317–339. https://doi.org/10.5169/seals-814104

Hervouet, R. (2019). A political ethnography of rural communities under an authoritarian regime: The case of Belarus. *BMS Bulletin of Sociological Methodology/ Bulletin De Methodologie Sociologique, 141*(1), 85–112. https://doi.org/10.1177/0759106318812790

Holmes, S. (2013). 'Is it worth risking your life?': Ethnography, risk and death on the U.S.-Mexico Border. *Social Science and Medicine, 99*, 153–161. https://doi.org/10.1016/j.socscimed.2013.05.029

Manos, I. (2010). Fieldwork on the border: Ethnographic engagements in South-Eastern Europe. In H. Donnan & T. M. Wilson (Eds.), *Borderlands: Ethnographic approaches to security, power and identity* (pp. 109–124). University Press of America.

Milligan, L. (2016). Insider-outsider-inbetweener? Researcher positioning, participative methods and cross-cultural educational research. *Compare, 46*(2), 235–250. https://doi.org/10.1080/03057925.2014.928510

Osman, W. (2020). *Television and the Afghan culture wars brought to you by foreigners, warlords, and activists.* University of Illinois Press.

Paillé, P., & Mucchielli, A. (2016). *L'analyse Qualitative En Sciences Humaines et Sociales.* Armand Colin.

Patton, M. (1990). *Qualitative evaluation and research methods.* Sage Publications.

Remtilla, A. (2012). *Re-producing social relations: Political and economic change and Islam in Post-Soviet Ishkashim.* PhD Thesis, University of Manchester.

Sadozaï, M. (2021a). Interview with Zalmaï, Conducted in Paris, 1 February 2021a (FR). *The Journal of Power Institutions in Post-Soviet Societies, 22.* https://doi.org/10.4000/pipss.6191

Sadozaï, M. (2021b). The Tajikistani-Afghan Border in Gorno-Badakhshan: Resources of a War-Orn Neighborhood. *Journal of Borderlands Studies,* 1–25. https://doi.org/10.1080/08865655.2021.1948798

Shih, V. (2015). Research in authoritarian regimes: Transparency tradeoffs and solutions. *Qualitative & Multi-Method Research, 13*, 20–22. https://doi.org/10.5281/zenodo.893087

Sluka, J. (1990). Participant observation in violent social contexts. *Human Organization, 49*(2), 114–126. https://doi.org/10.17730/humo.49.2.h033174683462676

Steck, J.-F. (2012). Etre Sur Le Terrain, Faire Du Terrain. *Hypothèses, 1*(15), 75–84.

Sultanalieva, S. (2022). Journalist's Jail Term Paints Dire Picture of Civil Rights in Tajikistan. *OpenDemocracy,* December 19. https://www.opendemocracy.net/en/odr/ulfatkhonim-mamadshoeva-jailed-tajikistan-journalist/

Thajib, F., Dinkelaker, S., & Stodulka, T. (2019). Introduction: Affective dimensions of fieldwork and ethnography. In T. Stodulka, S. Dinkelaker, & F. Thajib (Eds.), *Affective dimensions of fieldwork and ethnography* (pp. 7–20). Springer. https://doi.org/10.1080/14442213.2021.2020890

Thibault, H. (2021). 'Are you married?': Gender and faith in political ethnographic research. *Journal of Contemporary Ethnography, 50*(3), 395–416. https://doi.org/10.1177/0891241620986852

Thibault, H. (2023). Preface. In J. Dall'Agnola, A. Edwards, & M. Howlett (Eds.), Researching in the Former Soviet Union. Stories from the field (pp. iX-Xiii). London: Routledge.

Mélanie Sadozaï is a post-doctoral fellow at the Institute for European, Russian, and Eurasian Studies (IERES) of the George Washington University (2022–2023). She received her Ph.D. in Political Science and International Relations from the National Institute of Oriental Languages and Civilizations (INALCO/Sorbonne Paris Cité) in Paris, France. Her work, based on ethnographic methods and extensive fieldwork since 2014, focuses on cross-border relations in the remote areas of Afghanistan and Tajikistan in the Pamirs. She has published academic pieces in the *Journal of Borderlands Studies*, the *Journal of Power Institutions in Post-Soviet Societies* and *Problems of Post-Communism*.

Open Access This chapter is licensed under the terms of the Creative Commons Attribution 4.0 International License (http://creativecommons.org/licenses/by/4.0/), which permits use, sharing, adaptation, distribution and reproduction in any medium or format, as long as you give appropriate credit to the original author(s) and the source, provide a link to the Creative Commons license and indicate if changes were made.

The images or other third party material in this chapter are included in the chapter's Creative Commons license, unless indicated otherwise in a credit line to the material. If material is not included in the chapter's Creative Commons license and your intended use is not permitted by statutory regulation or exceeds the permitted use, you will need to obtain permission directly from the copyright holder.

Chapter 7
A Stranger in the Village: Anti-blackness in the Field

Alexa Kurmanov

Abstract In 1951, James Baldwin visited the remote town of Leukerbad, Switzerland, which inspired his essay *Stranger in the Village*. Baldwin's reflection of himself as a "first" encounter with Black flesh offers a critical reflection on overlooked discussions of the fatigue that accompanies Black researchers conducting fieldwork in (post)socialist spaces. In this chapter, I reflect on the ways my Black non-binary body becomes fatigued at the intersections of blackness and sexuality in the context of contemporary Kyrgyzstan. Furthermore, I address the sedimented representations of blackness that I embody, and the interactions my embodied (mis)representations invite, pushing us to think beyond the physicality of anti-blackness and to consider its psychological effects.

Keywords Central Asia · Kyrgyzstan · Anti-blackness · Black fatigue · (Post)socialist

Introduction

Midway through 2022, I anxiously awaited Jessica Nabongo's book *The Catch Me If You Can: One Woman's Journey to Every Country in the World.* I was a follower of Nabongo's Instagram account and eagerly anticipated reading about her travel as a Black woman through contemporary Central Asia. Her shaved head was important to me, because the combination of my bare scalp and being Black provoked unique and trying interactions with people in Kyrgyzstan. Recently, there has been an emerging genre of Black travel narratives on digital platforms like TikTok, YouTube, and Instagram. These accounts show the complexity of being Black and abroad, many times as a way to encourage Black people in America to explore life's possibilities outside

A. Kurmanov (✉)
University of California, Berkeley, CA, USA
e-mail: alexa_kurmanova@berkeley.edu

© The Author(s) 2024
J. Dall'Agnola and A. Sharshenova (eds.), *Researching Central Asia*,
SpringerBriefs in Political Science,
https://doi.org/10.1007/978-3-031-39024-1_7

of the United States. It serves as a digital Green Book[1] that clues Black populations into the scale of anti-blackness and racism they may encounter in particular countries (Klassen et al., 2022). However, before Nabongo and the emergence of digital Black travel narratives, it was nearly impossible to understand the complexity of being Black in Central Asia from a distance.

Before my first trip to Russia in 2018 and then Kyrgyzstan in 2019, I would search YouTube and other social media sites for guidance on how to navigate the social landscape. Often, these searches brought frustration because videos and blogs were limited to white men or white couples traveling through Kyrgyzstan. When I did locate the channels of Black vloggers, their explorations occluded Eurasia, especially Central Asia. Moreover, I could not see a reflection of myself, because many Black vloggers adorned themselves with "loose" wavy curls, braids, sew-ins, quick weaves, twist-outs, and seemed to neatly fit into (mis)representations of Black femininity. Although people are generally aware that blackness is not a monolith, and that race is not biological but a socially constructed reality, in the context of Kyrgyzstan, I embody various symbols of what Black *is* and is *not*. Aside from being visibly Black, I am queer and non-binary, which is at times revealed through my perceived gender expression. I say "perceived" because I am not openly non-binary or queer while in fieldwork, but nonetheless people project their own conceptualizations of gender and sex onto my body due to my shaved head and small physical frame. Thus, my positionality in fieldwork becomes deeply intertwined with inquiries in my research about the malleability and the fixedness of race, gender, sexuality, and their intersections and embodiment across space and time.

While reading Nabongo's short chapter on Kyrgyzstan, I was reminded of the persistence of stereotypes about blackness through the tensions of being a person's "first" encounter with Black flesh. On her walk to a mobile store to pick up a local sim card, she writes:

> I often forget in many places that I stand out like a sore thumb. As Nazira and I walked to the mobile shop, I noticed traffic literally stop and people staring at me. I thought to myself, Oh yeah, I'm Black. I was a rarity in this region. Most people in the country, and especially in the countryside, had probably never seen a Black person in real life. It's a surreal experience to be someone's first. I felt both very aware of the eyes on me and also that the people staring were more fascinated than malicious. (Nabongo, 2022, 233)

I empathized with her experience but also wondered if the stares were a combination of her closely shaved head and Black femmeness, as was the negative attention I experienced on previous trips abroad to Central Asia and Russia. In Nabongo's account, I was reminded of the oscillation between rage and pleasantness in James Baldwin's fatiguing encounters with curious inhabitants in a remote village in the Swiss Alps. Both Nabongo and Baldwin's "first" encounters invited inquiry into blackness as

---

[1] The Green Book was a publication that offered a variety of resources to Black travelers from 1936 to 1966. Some of these resources included Black-friendly businesses, travel stories, civil rights advocacy, and guidance on safe traveling. Many scholars are (re)thinking and critically examining digital spaces as newer iterations of the Green Book, for instance, digital spaces such as Black Twitter.

both a subject and a question (Rankine, 2016). In short, what chaos ensues when blackness is the centre of inquiry? How did my body either "problematize" (Bey, 2020) or collapse into monolithic notions of blackness more broadly and American blackness in particular? What are the consequences of this ongoing antagonism?

This chapter is an inquiry into the tensions of being someone's *first*. I invoke James Baldwin's (1955) essay *Stranger in the Village* to point to cases of Black fatigue produced by naïve forms of anti-black and anti-gender logic in fieldwork. I engage Mary Frances-Winters definition of Black Fatigue, which she states is the "repeated variations of stress that result in extreme exhaustion and are caused by mental, physical, and spiritual maladies that are passed from generation to generation" (2020, 33). This definition is based on the secondary meaning of fatigue, which involves the weakening of an object through repeated variations of stress. In short Frances-Winters' notion of Black fatigue posits how physically, mentally, and emotionally taxing systemic and everyday racism is for Black people in the context of the United States. Because Frances-Winters' definition of Black fatigue is shaped by the sociohistorical context of colonialism and racism in America, I use Baldwin's experiences to expand her notion of Black fatigue internationally and to reflect on how naivety and curiosity about Blackness can leave "microscopic pinpricks" (Khanga & Jacoby, 1992, 23). Another important concept in the context of Black fatigue is the concept of anti-blackness. Anti-blackness is defined as the "beliefs, attitudes, actions, practices, and behaviors of individuals and institutions that devalue, minimize, and marginalize the full participation of Black people" (Comrie et al., 2023, 74).

I am aware that, by reflecting on Black fatigue and anti-blackness in fieldwork and its consequences, I risk reproducing a particular kind of "discourse of danger" (Heathershaw & Megoran, 2011, 589) in the context of the Black experience abroad. Make no mistake, Kyrgyzstan has become a second home, and in many ways relieves me from the systemic racism of the United States. However, that does not mean that anti-blackness does not exist in the "social fabric" of geographies *peripherised* by Europe and the United States (Baldwin, 1955). My goals in this essay are, therefore, twofold. First, I aim to start a dialogue about being a Black researcher and student in the context of fieldwork in Central Asia. And second, I would like to turn attention to the innocence or "sublime ignorance" Black researchers and students encounter. My hope is that my experiences presented in this essay will not deter academic inquiry into Central Asia but be a tool for future Black researchers to think about their own positionality, at times as One-Third World (Mohanty, 2003, 226), as they navigate fieldwork.

Being One's First

In July 2019, Aliyu Tijjani Abubakar, a 38-year-old Nigerian man who lived and worked in Bishkek as the director of an English language school, was killed on the street near a local shopping centre (*Zum Aichurok*). Aliyu was on a video call with his wife when he noticed a young Kyrgyz man following him around and taking a video.

The two men got into a verbal altercation afterward, which ultimately led to Abubakar being struck in the face and consequently hitting his head on the pavement—he died after being in a coma for a few days (Djanibekova, 2019). When I heard about Aliyu Abubakar, I had been in Kyrgyzstan for less than a month on a program funded through the US Department of State. Upset by the news of Abubakar's murder, I reached out to my in-country program coordinator to discuss my anxiety about latent racism. She responded, using the logic of color blindness embedded in former nationality policies like *Korenizatsiia* (indigenization) and other policies like *druzhba narodov* (Russian term for "friendship of peoples") during the Soviet period. "There is no racism here. Kyrgyz people are not racists," she said.

I had heard a similar remark from in-country coordinators and instructors while abroad in Russia and Cuba. I was often accused of imposing my "American" view because the concept of race (for them) simply was non-existent in those spaces; thus, so were racism and anti-blackness. What struck me and upset me about Abubakar's death was the moment that led up to it. It was impossible for me to read it as anything other than a fetishistic curiosity and inquiry into the Black body, which resulted in Abubakar's assertiveness in protecting his personal boundaries. And, although his death sparked a tense debate about the existence of growing racist sentiments in Kyrgyz society, which reified the idea of racism as a foreign import, the sedimented experiences of Black fatigue that I had already experienced in the moments of "first" encounters left me unconvinced that his death was a random occurrence. July is the hottest month in Kyrgyzstan, especially in Bishkek, and even more so on the corner of *Shopokov Ulitsia* and *Chuy Prospekt*—tensions are running high. Abubakar lived in Bishkek for more than a decade. No doubt this was not the first time that someone had followed him around with their camera phone erect or snapping a photo, which to me solidified Abubakar's position as always and forever a "stranger" or as a "wonder" (Baldwin, 1955, 166). Although these exoticizing encounters can be seen as innocent and (at times) endearing, at their core, they are dehumanizing. In Baldwin's encounters with the people of Leukerbad, their curiosity about his physical characteristics, which were the source of much pain in the context of America, saw these as both infernal and miraculous but never human. He recounts their comments about his hair as the "color of tar" (Baldwin, 1955, 166) and its texture like wire or cotton. While these comments were a basis for genuine wonder, they misrecognized Baldwin's humanity. "I knew that they did not mean to be unkind and I know it now; it is necessary, nevertheless, for me to repeat this to myself each time I walk out of the chalet" (Bladwin, 1955, 166). Black Fatigue is present in Baldwin's "first" encounters with the people of Leukerbad. However, Baldwin felt that he could not hold them accountable for "what history is doing or has done" (Baldwin, 1955, 168). His oscillation between pleasantness and rage points to an active but slow fatiguing, an exoticizing of the Black body through gazing, naming, and touching.

Similar to Baldwin, my fieldwork was and continues to be filled with a variety of contentious "firsts" and the performance of "pleasantness" that involves carrying within the body the awkward weight of representation. Although the people of Leukerbad were aware that he was American, his Black body remained inevitably tied to a distorted image of Africa. "Everyone…knows that I come from America—though they will never really believe: black [people] come from Africa" (Baldwin, 1955, 165). Inquiries about my "real" birthplace have previously reopened wounds and reminded me that I am indeed a "stranger"—even in Africa. "Where are you *really* from?" I am from Chicago. Yes, but where are you *from*? This question, in particular, is loaded because it requires undoing the idea of Africa as a monolith—a continent seen as devoid of complexity. At times, I have had difficult but fruitful conversations that have come out of inquiries about my African heritage. For instance, on a taxi ride to Bishkek from the mountains, a couple inquired about my birthplace, and after giving a condensed lecture on the Atlantic Slave Trade, the husband then asked why I felt it important to travel to Kyrgyzstan when I should be traveling to Africa and help my African brothers? Although I took that opportunity to debunk the stereotype of Africa as "primitive" and "depraved" and soon shifted the conversation to his own views of colonial practice in Central Asia, I exited that conversation mentally and emotionally exhausted. Like Baldwin, I was aware that I could not hold him responsible for what he had unconsciously inherited (Baldwin, 1955, 168). Not only have historical processes of racism and colonialism deployed "thousands of details, anecdotes, and stories" about blackness, it continues to do so on a global scale through various forms of digital media and the consumption of blackness as a commodity.

Black Fatigue and Anti-blackness

Often the entwinement between blackness, gender, and sexuality redresses my body as unintelligible. This is because I simply do not embody mainstream representations of Black femininity, which make Black women's bodies legible. My shaved head (i.e., gender expression) betrays me, making me unable to live up to Black femininity—which is tied to hair—and all its excess. The reactions I get as a result of my hair and other parts of my body in fieldwork show just how paradoxical blackness can be. Suggestions about my inherent ability at physical activity, good sex, dancing, and singing are present in everyday conversations with complete strangers. My hair, which carries the particular weight and trauma of white supremacist logic in the context of the United States, frequently causes confusion about my gender. I do not "look" like the mainstream representations of Black women—Naomi Campbell, Beyonce, or Cardi B. I am flat-chested, short, and bald, but have been called some of these names because of my being both American and Black. Simultaneously, I have been called a gay man on the street. I have been both laughed at and complimented while walking with friends and family. Through the years, these instances have revealed to me that for many of the people I encounter in fieldwork, there is an inability to recognize my humanity. I am a reconfigured variant of a "controlling image" in highly marketable Black popular culture where ideas about Black sexuality are consistently "reformulated and contested" (Hill, 2004, 121.) However, like Baldwin,

I feel that I cannot hold them accountable for what history is doing and what it has done.

The experiences of being seen as a stranger are not unfamiliar to many Black people in America. And despite experiences that manifest in a variety of forms, such as microaggressions, overt racism, and systemic racism, that many Black Americans are subject to every day, whenever I tell someone that I am going abroad, they ask me if it's safe for "us." Meaning "Us" as in us Black people. My family usually tells me, with genuine concern and care to "be careful" and "stay safe" because of what they've heard about other global contexts. These interactions are not unique. Other Black scholars who do research in (post)socialist spaces have had the same conversations with family (St. Julian-Varnon, 2020). In fact, the inception of the blog *chernyy kleb*[2] (Russian for 'black bread'), a site created by Imani Crawford, was made to ease her family's anxieties about her safety as a Black woman abroad. She has since repurposed her blog as a pedagogical tool to help dispel "discourses of danger" pertaining to anti-blackness and racism that reproduce the idea that the United States is safer for Black people than other countries. Jessica Nabongo's use of Malcolm X, invites us to consider how white supremacist logic enmeshed in "discourses of danger" continues to affect the mobility of Black bodies:

> American propaganda is designed to make us think that no matter how much hell we catch here, we are still better off in America than we would be anywhere else. (Malcom X)

The fear of anti-blackness elsewhere has stopped many Black Americans from traveling abroad, and this includes Black researchers and students. The anxiety about anti-blackness and racism abroad is also coupled with systemic racism at "home" through access to privileges of travel. I did not receive my first passport until I was 26 years old.[3] And, similar to so many other Black researchers and students, when I finally traveled abroad, I rarely received adequate emotional support. Often, cohorts for study abroad programs were predominately white. The discussions at the orientations, both stateside and in-country, were a reflection of the cohort and was undergirded with the assumption that the experiences of students and researcher were universal—which meant White men/women. Furthermore, I found that, although I was physically outside of America, some students had carried a particular grain of American racism with them abroad, which was evident in their interactions with me and with the local community. Black fatigue was not only caused by interactions of inquiry about my body in the field but also by the complex makeup of the American cohort I was with. Moreover, this is compounded by the inability of the academic institution to recognize anti-blackness beyond the physical, as a practice that operates through a variety of other modalities, including academic institutions and state-funded programs that applaud themselves for being "diverse."

---

[2] For more details please visit the following website: https://blackbread.org/.

[3] The only way I was able to access a passport was through the CIEE passport caravan that came to the University of Pittsburgh in 2018. The caravan's mission was to support students who have been historically underrepresented in study abroad programs.

Conclusion

While the context of Baldwin's 1953 essay, set in the remote village of Leukerbad, Switzerland, is vastly different from that of contemporary Kyrgyzstan, in this essay, I find commonality in his encounter with the local population. The differences are not only temporal but also racial, ethnic, historical, and cultural. Leukerbad is a predominately White Swiss space, and Kyrgyzstan is a multi-ethnic (post)socialist and (post)colonial country. For me, this makes the question of *how* and *where* anti-blackness appears even more pertinent. What I like most about Baldwin's analysis is that his status as a "stranger" in the village, which serves as a critique of White supremacy, does not essentialize racism in one context over another but blurs the geographical boundaries of anti-blackness. In other words, he is not only a stranger in Leukerbad but also at home in America. This point is key. One can thus step out of the racial matrix of the United States, perhaps in a search for a moment of reprieve, and still find that the "markers" that overdetermine their body follow them to other contexts, even in places with a history of "anti-racist" and "anti-colonial" policies (Spillers, 1987).

As a Black researcher who embodies various "markers" and who constantly questions and criticizes how race is discursively constructed and reified (Hall, 2017), I find that academic institutions are still failing to identify Black fatigue as an outcome of mundane encounters in fieldwork. Moreover, anti-blackness is not only limited to people of African descent in the United States or Europe but is prevalent in global contexts through logics of colorism, which privileges proximity to whiteness. Anti-blackness is not always explicit but can be practiced implicitly in the everyday. My hope is that my reflections presented here will draw more attention to how we *all* (not just Black scholars and scholars of color) can be equipped to be more supportive in cases in which anti-blackness is not always evident. Similar to others, I believe that we are on the right track toward supporting emerging Black scholars, but many programs and institutions overlook elementary forms of White supremacy that take place in fieldwork or study abroad.

References

Baldwin, J. (1955). *Notes of a native son*. Beacon Press.
Bey, M. (2020). *The problem of the Negro as a problem for gender*. University of Minnesota Press.
Comrie, W., Landor, A., Riley, T., & Williamson, J. (2023). Anti-Blackness/Colorism. Available here: https://www.bu.edu/antiracism-center/files/2022/06/Anti-Black.pdf
Djanibekova, N. (2019). Kyrgyzstan: Killing of Nigerian Teacher Sparks Conversation Around Racism. *Eurasianet*, July 10. https://eurasianet.org/kyrgyzstan-killing-of-nigerian-teacher-sparks-conversation-around-racism
Hall, S. (2017). In K. Mercer (Ed.), *The fateful triangle: Race, ethnicity, nation*. Harvard University Press.

Heathershaw, J., & Megoran, N. (2011). Contesting danger: A new agenda for policy and scholarship on Central Asia. *International Affairs, 87*(3), 589–612. https://doi.org/10.1111/j.1468-2346.2011.00992.x

Hill, C. (2004). *Black sexual politics: African Americans, Gender, and the New Racism*. Routledge.

Khanga, Y., & Jacoby, S. (1992). *Soul to Soul: A Black Russian American Family, 1865–1992*. W.W. Norton.

Klassen, S., Kingsley, S., McCall, K., Weinberg, J., & Fiesler, C. (2022). Black lives, green books, and blue checks: Comparing the content of the Negro Motorist Green Book to the Content on Black Twitter. Proceedings of the ACM on human-computer interaction 6, no. GROUP: 1–22.

Mohanty, C. T. (2003). *Feminism without borders: Decolonizing theory, practicing solidarity*. Duke University Press.

Nabongo, J. (2022). *The catch me if you can: One woman's journey to every country in the world*. National Geographic Society.

Rankine, C. (2016). A New Grammar for Blackness. *Aperture*, September 22. https://aperture.org/editorial/new-grammar-blackness/

Spillers, H. (1987). Mama's baby, papa's maybe: An American Grammar Book. *Diacritics, 17*(2), 65–81. https://doi.org/10.2307/464747

St. Julian-Varnon, K. (2020). A voice from the Slavic Studies Edge: On being a Black woman in the field. *NewsNet ASEEES, 60*(4), 1–4. https://www.aseees.org/news-events/aseees-blog-feed/voice-slavic-studies-edge-being-black-woman-field

Winters, M. (2020). *Black fatigue: How racism erodes the mind, body, and spirit* (1st ed.). Berrett-Koehler Publishers Inc.

Alexa Kurmanov is a doctoral candidate in the Anthropology Department at the University of California, Berkeley. Broadly their research focuses on LGBT and feminist activism in Kyrgyzstan through the lens of Black feminist theorization and methods of intersectionality. In particular, they explore the ways in which the category of "woman" in (post)socialist/(post)colonial Kyrgyzstan is reconstructed by state and public discourse. Furthermore, how the category of "woman" cuts through class, race, and space and how local LGBT and feminist communities navigate, contest, and rearticulate notions of gender and sex in the everyday.

Open Access This chapter is licensed under the terms of the Creative Commons Attribution 4.0 International License (http://creativecommons.org/licenses/by/4.0/), which permits use, sharing, adaptation, distribution and reproduction in any medium or format, as long as you give appropriate credit to the original author(s) and the source, provide a link to the Creative Commons license and indicate if changes were made.

The images or other third party material in this chapter are included in the chapter's Creative Commons license, unless indicated otherwise in a credit line to the material. If material is not included in the chapter's Creative Commons license and your intended use is not permitted by statutory regulation or exceeds the permitted use, you will need to obtain permission directly from the copyright holder.

Part III
Doing Research in Closed Contexts

Chapter 8
Safety, Security, and Self-Censorship as Survival Strategies

Aijan Sharshenova

Abstract In this paper, I will discuss concerns of safety and security, and the resulting reluctant self-censorship as one of the many realities associated with the work of a political scientist in Kyrgyzstan. In doing so, I will combine the existing research on self-censorship and working in non-democratic environments with self-reflection as a local political scientist. In particular, this contribution dives into the intangible fear felt by researchers, who find themselves making difficult decisions on a daily basis, where personal security is an object of continuous and sometimes perceived negotiation with an invisible enemy.

Keywords Central Asia · Political science · Self-censorship · Authoritarian environment

Introduction

In December 2021, I was participating in an online political discussion on the recent parliamentary elections in Kyrgyzstan when the doorbell rang. At first, it was merely a loud noise that distracted me for a fraction of a moment, but few seconds later, I froze in fear. I was staying in a friend's flat in central Bishkek as I was doing an extensive renovation in my own flat that winter. Nobody knew I was there apart from my friend, the flat owner. She never came unannounced. It was after 11 p.m. Bishkek time. This was hardly the time for the mailman, head of condominium, salespeople, local mosque activists, or any other person who was likely to knock on your door without a formal invitation. I carried on with the discussion as if nothing had happened but checked the door afterwards and messaged the landlady to check whether it was her (it was not). I did my best to push away and disregard my fear, but struggled to figure out why this doorbell ring had gotten me so scared. Deep down,

---

A. Sharshenova (✉)
OSCE Academy Bishkek, Bishkek, Kyrgyzstan
e-mail: a.sharshenova@osce-academy.net

© The Author(s) 2024
J. Dall'Agnola and A. Sharshenova (eds.), *Researching Central Asia*,
SpringerBriefs in Political Science,
https://doi.org/10.1007/978-3-031-39024-1_8

I probably knew I was worried that my work as a political scientist might affect my safety and security, but was not ready to face those gnawing concerns.

In this chapter, I engage with the existing literature on both non-local (Dall'Agnola, 2023b; Gentile, 2013; Glasius et al., 2018; Menga, 2020) and local researcher (Janenova, 2019; Norov *in this edited volume*) positionality and on doing research in non-democratic environments, and discuss how the shrinking space for rights and academic freedoms in Central Asia informs researchers' choices of what to say and what not to say. When we research and speak about our places of origin, we have to consider a variety of concerns. It could be public shame at the societal level that researchers might face (Kudaibergenova, 2019), or the very real threat of repression, physical safety concerns (see more in the next chapter by Norov and in Antonov et al., 2021), and/or post-colonial and neo-imperial hierarchies of knowledge production (Kim, 2019a), which shape our professional paths.

My experiences, as well as fears, concerns, and survival strategies, might not necessarily be shared by all fellow researchers, but they might be something some of my colleagues, and especially those who are local to the region, can relate to. While acknowledging that this is potentially an uncomfortable topic to discuss in an expert community, I am convinced it is important to raise the issues of safety and security of local researchers and explore how it affects their choices around self-censorship.

Safety and Security Concerns

In June 2022, while browsing through Kyrgyz newsfeeds as per my daily ritual, I stumbled upon a piece of news that shook me to the core: My former Applied Politics lecturer, Professor Marat Kazakpaev, had died in hospital after 14 months' detention in a Kyrgyzstan Security Services detention facility (also known by its Russian abbreviation as SIZO GKNB) on high treason charges (Radio Free Europe/Radio Liberty, 2022). A few days after Kazapaev's death, the head of security services, Kamchibek Tashiev, gave a long interview to the *Litsa* (Russian term for "faces") media outlet (Litsa, 2022). Tashiev stated that the security services had nothing to do with Kazakpaev's untimely death and that they "did everything to save him" (Litsa, 2022). Tashiev shifted the blame for Kazakpaev's death to the medical council, which had released him back to the temporary detention facility after a medical examination and the pressure of being locked up in detention. While he was alive, Kazakpaev requested that the Ombudsman's office investigate the case of his detention and insisted that he was persecuted for his expert opinion on the Security Services' border management policies (Ombudsman's Office, 2022). Similar opinions were expressed by other political observers in April 2022 soon after the detention of the political scientist (Nurmatov, 2021).

I did not stay in touch with Professor Kazakpaev after my graduation as life got in the way of maintaining any social relationships of the past. I doubt he would even remember me as we, politics and international relations students, were many. But I always remembered him as one of the most knowledgeable, professional, and competent educators in my undergraduate university. Professor Kazakpaev was truly passionate about his subject—Politics—and shared his knowledge, passion, and experience generously with his students.

His death was shocking to both civil society and academia in Kyrgyzstan as it was every local and regional political expert's worst nightmare—persecution for doing our jobs. This was my deep-seated, bottled fear too. It made me slower, less open, often reluctant to share my work or opinions publicly or even behind the closed doors. I have learnt to consider every word carefully, to speak less, to alternate sensitive topics such as the questionable policy choices of the ruling elites with something less "dangerous" like post-Soviet nostalgia, and to take breaks from analytical work and do something else, something less public, like teaching research methods or doing project management jobs.

Safety concerns are very much real for Central Asian researchers. Doing research in more "closed" environments is an emerging body of literature, which often focuses on access to information and fieldwork. Some literature has focused on cooperation, networks, and research framing as a way to navigate safety and security issues (Bekmurzaev et al., 2018). Other publications have focused on a variety of dilemmas associated with doing research in authoritarian environments (Dall'Agnola, 2023b; Gentile, 2013; Glasius et al., 2018; Janenova, 2019). Doing research in seemingly democratic regions seems to have deep-seated and often invisible challenges too, which often remain under-researched.

These challenges relate to physical safety, integrity, social position, financial stability, visibility, and many other factors which contribute to hushing, devaluation, and erasure of the voices of local Central Asian researchers from public domains at the local, regional, and global levels. Norov, in this book (see next chapter), provides a chilling account of how security services can suppress, silence, and even recruit local researchers to promote pro-government narratives or spy on fellow researchers. Antonov et al. (2021) explored the concepts of suppression, acquiescence, and incorporation of academics into the service of an authoritarian state in certain depth. Norov's and Antonov et al. (2021) reflections on the state of academic freedom in Central Asia certainly resonate with my personal experiences, albeit (thankfully) not to the same extent.

Persecution of academics is not a recent phenomenon. The Central Asia Political Exile (CAPE) database compiled by a research team at the University of Exeter lists at least two academics who had to flee their countries due to grave security concerns as early as the 1990s (Exeter Central Asian Studies Network, 2023). Turkmen historian and journalist Shokhrat Kadyrov had to flee his country in 1993, at the dawn of Turkmenistan's independence. Given how the political situation led to one of the most oppressive political regimes in the world, his decision was probably the most suitable one.

Safety concerns are very much linked to the positionality of each researcher. Positionality can be defined in various ways, but largely refers to how a person's multilayered identity shapes and informs their relations with others (Dall'Agnola, 2023a). Safety concerns can be very different depending on a researcher's positionality and their field or area of study. For example, the concerns of foreign researchers in the field might be very different from the concerns of local researchers. After all, a foreign researcher might be able to leave the field if the field gets too dangerous or uncomfortable. For a local researcher, removing themselves physically, intellectually, and emotionally from the field is almost unimaginable because the field is home, where everything we care about is.

In addition, female researchers potentially have to take more precautions and develop more sophisticated safety protocols when doing research compared to their male colleagues (Turlubekova, 2023). Security goes beyond physical safety as it can refer to a range of aspects that affect our sense of fear and absence of real or perceived threats. Security can thus refer to and be associated with physical integrity, mental well-being, financial stability, and many other factors which affect our ability to live, work, and function.

Being a female local researcher is accompanied with a wide range of visible and invisible safety and security threats and concerns. At the most fundamental level, female researchers, foreign and local alike, have to take into consideration their physical safety and well-being (see chapter by Dall'Agnola in this book). Other aspects of being a female local researcher can vary across disciplines, career levels, regional knowledge production domains, and many other factors. For example, female academics in Central Asia can face a very considerable pay gap, which might affect their financial security and empowerment (as reported by Suyarkulova, 2019). Or, if they find themselves in early career positions, they could be required under threat of dismissal to share their intellectual products with their seniors (as told by Kim, 2019a). Injustice and inequality (including inequality rooted in the colonial past, see Marat & Aisarina, 2021), as well as alienation and loneliness (both literal and professional), are very much real and not often discussed publicly. Coupled with fears for physical safety, potential societal and state persecution, and shaming, it makes it much more difficult for a female researcher to be heard, taken into account, and listened to.

In my case, being a female political analyst has brought me an unexpected, albeit very thin, level of safety. Women can be disregarded in a traditional patriarchal society and, in my very specific case, it gives me less visibility where I want to have it. Unlike my fellow male political commentors like Norov or Kazakpaev, I am less visible and less likely to be taken seriously by security services or those in power back home.

Nevertheless, to secure both my physical and mental well-being in a more closely monitored society, I have adopted several preventive mechanisms. First, I made an effort to build an extensive professional network of both local and foreign colleagues who might (or might not, as it is their right, not their duty) help me reach out and make my plea visible in the worst-case scenario. As a young researcher, I closely followed the fate of Tajik political scientist Alexander Sodiqov, who was detained during his fieldwork at home in Tajikistan. His friends and colleagues made his case visible (see Heathershaw, 2014), signed a petition, and eventually managed to get him out of the country. I learnt from Sodiqov's case and did my best to stay in regular touch with like-minded people around the world. I also made sure not to be publicly visible when talking to foreign researchers: When meeting with a foreign colleague in a public space, I tend to face a wall and keep my face away from any incoming human traffic. This is to ensure I am not accused of conspiring with foreigners. Unfortunately, law enforcement and security services can be very blind when they want to and might ignore that these foreigners are PhD students, who might struggle to buy me a cup of coffee, let alone purchase some state secrets (to which I do not have any access, just to make this clear[1]). Similar to other local female scholars (Turlubekova, 2023), I have also adopted a habit of reporting my location and day plan to my family when engaged in fieldwork, interviews, or any other work-related travel. This is a habit I fostered as a solo female traveler and it is there to ensure somebody who cares about me knows where to start looking for me if I disappear. In everyday life, I have adopted the practice of self-censorship, which accompanies me in my daily professional and personal lives.

Self-Censorship

In April 2023, I got invited to give oral evidence in front of the Foreign Affairs Committee in the Parliament of the United Kingdom. As someone who has hardly ever been invited to their own country's parliament in the capacity of an expert, I was certainly very honored. It felt like I had achieved something—if nothing else, I had made myself visible and heard as both a Central Asian and Central Asianist. However, once the initial excitement subsided, my thinking turned toward what I might be asked about and what I should say. Thankfully, the committee hearing focused mainly on the UK's engagement with the region rather than the political situation in Central Asia, so I felt safe to share an open and honest expert opinion.

However, limitations to what we can and cannot say accompany local researchers researching Central Asia continuously. "Is this going to be recorded?" "Do you know who will attend this event?" "Who else will talk at the event?": These are probably a set of most frequently asked questions when one tries to organize an expert event on politics in Kyrgyzstan. Publications, participation in conferences, interviews, and even class discussions are subject to continuous internal negotiation between the aspiration to do our job well and the concern for our safety and security. Walking the fine line between keeping oneself safe and doing one's job in an open and honest manner is an exhausting challenge, which has probably pushed a number of brilliant researchers out of the profession in Central Asia.

Researchers arrive at the decision to self-censor due to a variety of reasons. Some would like to avoid criticism, dissension, and problems (Kim, 2019b, 64). Others observe the all-pervasive formal censorship (e.g., as described in Janenova, 2019) and have to factor that in when researching their field. Bekmurzaev provides an

---

[1] High treason or espionage are the most likely charges which could be used against an expert, a translator, a civil society activist, or anybody else working with foreigners, even though they are very unlikely to have access to classified information. For example, Marat Kazakpaev's charge was high treason—the details of his case are still not public.

account of how it struck him that he had to worry both for his research and its participants: "it became obvious to me that research on this topic and factors of conflict would provoke the authorities' interest and, in the worst case, lead to my research being obstructed and participants being endangered" (Bekmurzaev et al., 2018, 110). In some cases, self-censorship is dictated by the legal and normative frameworks of non-democratic countries, where states attempt to seize an increasing amount of control over knowledge production (Bekmurzaev et al., 2018, 102). Out of the fear of angering the local authorities, some local scholars see themselves forced to publish under a pen name, as Ruslan Norov's account in this book shows. In more democratic countries, legal systems are often used to censor too, albeit to serve the interests of businesses and elites rather than the state. For example, in the United Kingdom, the so-called SLAPPs—strategic lawsuits against public participation— have become one of the weapons of the wealthy to censor academic scholarship that does not serve their interests (Williams et al., 2020).

I learnt to self-censor very early in my career. My first publication in 2007 was in an academic journal issued by my undergraduate university press and focused on the state of democracy in Kyrgyzstan under President Bakiev, while President Bakiev was still in power. I hardly remember the process of writing that first academic publication. I do keep memories of that sticky feeling that I had to choose my words wisely and find a way to deliver my critical arguments and evidence without risking the paper not being published. It was probably a clumsily written and wishy-washy piece of work, but it was my first experience of public expression and self-censorship.

Since then, self-censorship has become a part of professional and personal life. In professional life, it informs what I publish and I how I express myself, which probably impedes me from holding more honest conversations with my potential readers and collocutors (e.g., podcast hosts or journalists). I publish less on politically sensitive topics for the same reason. It affects my personal digital life too: I possibly post only one in five tweets I actually write. My social media usage is limited for the same reason: Only Twitter is fairly open, the rest are rather hidden. I mostly write in English and avoid doing interviews or any other public appearances in Russian because I am less likely to be spotted by "those in power" if I speak in a language they do not normally use. My vanity has had to take a blow too: We have a newspaper in Kyrgyzstan which regularly publishes stories about Kyrgyzstanis who have made it abroad—achieved something in sciences, sports, or arts, or just managed to get a scholarship and get a prestigious Western education for free. I am not likely to ever get featured there because I actively hide myself from the gaze of the general public and the state back home.

Conclusion

Before June 2022, my personal perception was that academics and experts in Kyrgyzstan could be critical of the ruling elites to an extent as we were often disregarded by the authorities. Or, at least, one could test the ground and prod the limits of our "boldness." Kazakpaev's case prompted me to take an uncomfortable look into my deep-seated fear of potential persecution for any public expression of opinions. While these fears might never come true and might not be even real, given my limited visibility and capacity to make a real difference in Kyrgyzstan, these fears very much inform the application of self-censorship to my publications, my choice of communication formats and languages, and career decisions.

When Jasmin suggested we could put together a volume of essays on doing fieldwork and research in Central Asia, I thought it could be a chance to reflect on my fears and concerns, which might be shared by fellow political scientists, analysts, and other experts in Central Asia. Writing this chapter has been challenging to say the least, as once more, I had to choose what I could safely say. This book still feels like a "safe haven"—a space for free and open expression because it is an academic publication in the English language whose readers are more likely to be compassionate or non-violently critical.

A political scientist in Kyrgyzstan can choose a variety of career paths. Some choose to teach; others prefer to carry out academic or policy research. Quite a few of us combine both with public engagement in the form of media interviews, podcasts, and analytical and other publications. This part of our jobs requires us to speak up and to comment on politically sensitive events, trends, and political actors. Doing this part can come at a cost. Sometimes, it can be minor, for example, fleeting comments by your concerned fellows that you should probably be more careful when expressing your positions. Other times, it can be irreversible and incommensurate, and simply not worth it.

References

Antonov, A., Lemon, E., & Mullojonov, P. (2021). Academic freedom in Tajikistan: How the suppression, acquiesce and incorporation of intellectuals strengthens the state and affects knowledge production. *Central Asian Survey, 40*(4), 592–610. https://doi.org/10.1080/02634937.2021.1925631

Bekmurzaev, N., Lottholz, P., & Meyer, J. (2018). Navigating the safety implications of doing research and being researched in Kyrgyzstan: Cooperation, networks and framing. *Central Asian Survey, 37*(1), 100–118. https://doi.org/10.1080/02634937.2017.1419165

Dall'Agnola, J. (2023a). The challenges of fieldwork in Post-Soviet Societies. In J. Dall'Agnola, A. Edwards, & M. Howlett. (Eds.), Researching in the Former Soviet Union. Stories from the Field. BASEES/Routledge Series on Russian and East European Studies. https://doi.org/10.4324/9781003144168-1

Dall'Agnola, J. (2023b). Fieldwork under surveillance: A research note. *Surveillance & Society, 21*(2).

Exeter Central Asian Studies Network. (2023). CAPE: Database of Known Central Asian Political Exiles. Available at https://excas.net/exiles/. Accessed on 23 May 2023.

Gentile, M. (2013). Meeting the 'Organs': The Tacit Dilemma of field research in authoritarian states. *Area, 45*(4), 426–432. https://doi.org/10.1111/area.12030

Glasius, M., de Lange, M., Bartman, J., Dalmasso, E., Lv, A., Del Sordi, A., Michaelsen, M., & Ruijgrok, K. (2018). *Research, ethics and risk in the authoritarian field*. Palgrave Macmillan.

Heathershaw, H. (2014). Consequences of the detention of Alexander Sodiqov. *openDemocracy*, July 22. https://www.opendemocracy.net/en/odr/consequences-of-detention-of-alexander-sodiqov/

Janenova, S. (2019). The boundaries of research in an authoritarian state. *International Journal of Qualitative Methods, 18*, 1–8. https://doi.org/10.1177/1609406919876469

Kim, E. (2019a). On academic extortion and complaining as activism. *openDemocracy*, October 7. https://www.opendemocracy.net/en/odr/when-the-field-is-your-institution-on-academic-extortion-and-complaining-as-activism/

Kim, S.-M. (2019b). Criticizing motherland to foreigners. In E. Mawdsley, E. Fourie, and W. Nauta (Eds.), *Researching south–south development cooperation: The politics of knowledge production*. Routledge. https://doi.org/10.4324/9780429459146-6

Kudaibergenova, D. (2019). When your field is also your home: Introducing feminist subjectivities in Central Asia. *openDemocracy*, October 7. https://www.opendemocracy.net/en/odr/when-your-field-also-your-home-introducing-feminist-subjectivities-central-asia/

Litsa. (2022). O smerti Kazakpaeva, ob ugrozah Madumarovu, o presledovanii Temirova (English translation is "On Kazakpaev's death, on the threats received by Madumarov, and on oppression of Temirov"), Interview with Kamchibek Tashiev by Litsa media outlet, available at http://nlkg.kg/ru/interview/o-smerti-kazakpaeva_-ob-ugrozax-madumarovu_-o-presledovanii-temirova. Accessed on 23 May 2023.

Marat, E., & Z. Aisarina (2021). Towards a more equal field in Central Asia Research. *openDemocracy*, January 8. https://www.opendemocracy.net/en/odr/towards-more-equal-field-central-asia-research/

Menga, F. (2020). Researchers in the Panopticon? Geographies of research, fieldwork, and authoritarianism. *Geographical Review, 110*(3), 341–357. https://doi.org/10.1080/00167428.2019.1684197

Ombudsman's Office. (2022). Sotrudniki apparata Ombudsmana KR posetili SIZO GKNB, gde proveli vstrechu so sledstvenno-zaderzhannym Maratov Kazakpaevym (English translation is "Staff of the Kyrgyz Republic's Ombudsman visited Security Services' Detention Centre, where they met with the detained Marat Kazakpaev), available at the website of the Ombudsman's Office at https://bit.ly/3N2h8nL. Accessed on 23 May 2023.

Nurmatov, E. (2021). S chem svyazan arest podozrevaemogo v gozizmene politologa? *Radio Free Europe/Radio Liberty's Kyrgyz Service*, April 15. https://rus.azattyk.org/a/31204612.html

Radio Free Europe/Radio Liberty. (2022). Well-known Kyrgyz Political Analyst Dies While in Custody on High Treason Charge. *RFE/RL's Kyrgyz Service news*, June 10. https://www.rferl.org/a/kyrgyzstan-kazakpaev-dies-detention-treason/31892754.html

Suyarkulova, M. (2019). A view from the margins: Alienation and accountability in Central Asian Studies. *openDemocracy*, October 10. https://www.opendemocracy.net/en/odr/view-margins-alienation-and-accountability-central-asian-studies/

Turlubekova, Z. (2023). A woman of her word prepared for the worst: Researching drug trafficking in Kazakhstan. In J. Dall'Agnola, A. Edwards, & M. Howlett. (Eds.), *Researching in the Former Soviet Union. Stories from the Field*. BASEES/Routledge Series. https://doi.org/10.4324/9781003144168-11

Williams, N., Hueting, L., & Milewska, P. (2020). The increasing rise, and impact, of SLAPPs: Strategic Lawsuits Against Public Participation. *Foreign Policy Centre*, December 9. https://fpc.org.uk/the-increasing-rise-and-impact-of-slapps-strategic-lawsuits-against-public-participation

Aijan Sharshenova is a Bishkek-based political analyst and a Research Fellow at the OSCE Academy in Bishkek, the Foreign Policy Centre in London, and the European Neighbourhood Council in Brussels. She holds a Ph.D. in Politics awarded at the University of Leeds, UK. In addition to her academic background in international studies, she has worked at the UN and UNDP country offices in the Middle East. Her research interests include foreign policy, public diplomacy, democracy promotion, autocracy diffusion in Russia and Central Asia.

Open Access This chapter is licensed under the terms of the Creative Commons Attribution 4.0 International License (http://creativecommons.org/licenses/by/4.0/), which permits use, sharing, adaptation, distribution and reproduction in any medium or format, as long as you give appropriate credit to the original author(s) and the source, provide a link to the Creative Commons license and indicate if changes were made.

The images or other third party material in this chapter are included in the chapter's Creative Commons license, unless indicated otherwise in a credit line to the material. If material is not included in the chapter's Creative Commons license and your intended use is not permitted by statutory regulation or exceeds the permitted use, you will need to obtain permission directly from the copyright holder.

Chapter 9
Navigating Academic Repression in Central Asia

Ruslan Norov

Abstract While much has been written about the risks facing foreign researchers conducting fieldwork under the "watchful eyes" of the local authorities in Central Asia, personal accounts by local scholars are less common. In this chapter, I reflect on attempts by the local organs to suppress and silence my voice, as well as to recruit me to spread government propaganda. While doing so, I examine the various state-led threats to academic freedom and researcher safety. I also discuss how these threats have affected my ability to conduct research and what others can do to avoid or manage them.

Keywords Repression · Researcher safety · Collaboration · Surveillance

Introduction

One Autumn afternoon around a decade ago, I was invited for tea with the director of my institute at the Academy of Sciences. Such informal meetings occurred every few weeks. Usually, my boss would ask me about my research, who I was meeting with and my plans. As a historian who worked with foreign colleagues in Europe, North America and Japan, I was treated with suspicion by my colleagues. I entered my boss' spacious office and sat down. He poured the tea. Once the *piola* (Central Asian word for "tea bowl") was full, his tone changed. He began to angrily accuse me of espionage and cooperation with the intelligence services of foreign states. At first, he demanded that I admit my guilt and repent. When I refused, he came up close to me and, adopting a friendlier approach, asked me to cooperate with the security services as an informant. Seeing that I was not interested, he quickly switched to his more aggressive mode and began to threaten that "if this does not suit you, then you will be held criminally liable for treason". I objected and said that I had not committed any crime, and I was not going to cooperate with the security services. He responded that if I wanted to continue my work at the institute, I would have to

R. Norov (✉)
Stockholm, Sweden

cooperate with the security services and "voluntarily" write a statement that I agree to be a freelancer. I flatly refused. This would not remain the only time the local "organs" (Gentile, 2013, 428) tried to coerce me into working for them.

As my own personal story outlined above shows, although I have never been associated with any opposition group, political party or movement, the government considered me a potential spy and threat to their power. This is nothing new. Referring to China, Perry (2020) analyses the "scholar–state" nexus, exploring how authoritarian rule rests on the suppression of independent academics, the "educated acquiescence" (Perry, 2020, 2) of academia or their incorporation into the "factory of answers" (Roche, 2018, 93). Such methods severely restrict the kinds of research and knowledge local scholars can conduct, put their lives in danger and force many to exercise exit strategies or publicly declare loyalty (Hirschmann, 1970).

Apart from some very rare personal accounts where foreign researchers reflect on their fieldwork under the "watchful eyes" (Sökefeld & Strasser, 2016, 159) of the local authorities in Central Asia (Dall'Agnola, 2023; Gentile, 2013; Trevisani, 2016; Bekmurzaev et al., 2018) or in other "closed contexts" (Glasius et al., 2018; Koch, 2013), reflections of local scholars on their experiences/dealings with security agencies are generally missing, a product of the repression such reflections would undoubtedly describe. This is problematic because, when scholars are from Central Asia and do not have a status in a different country, the power dynamics are different. For that reason, in this essay, I reflect on attempts by the local organs to suppress and silence my voice, as well as to recruit me to spread government propaganda.

I grew up in the capital city of one of the five Central Asian countries.[1] As an independent-minded individual, I faced the authorities' pressure from a very early age, starting in 2005, when I first volunteered with an international organisation and later, when I started working with local NGOs as a trainer on youth policy. Moreover, I was a history teacher at one of the capital's schools and at one of the universities and, in the process of teaching, I urged my students to be critical of history, to develop a critical mind and to, therefore, not just blindly believe and follow the official rhetoric of the authorities and the ideology of the state. Subsequently, the State National Security Committee added me to its blacklist of enemies of the people, revisionists, spies, traitors and dissidents, a list on which I remain to this day. As a result, I fled the country and settled in Europe. While I continue my research, I do so, using a penname.

The remainder of the chapter uses my autoethnographic account to examine the restrictions on academic freedom and threats to researcher safety centred on three forms: repression, cooptation and collaboration.

---

[1] Due to the sensitivity of the topic, all names used in this account are pseudonyms. For the same reason, I decided to avoid mentioning the specific places, cities and countries in which I grew up, lived and worked in Central Asia.

Repression of Academic Freedom

Academic freedom is severely restricted across Central Asia. All the countries in the region are in the bottom third of the Academic Freedom Index (Kinzelbach et al., 2023). In this regard, over the past decade, the authorities have made persistent efforts to eradicate academic freedom and independent thought in the region. As a result, over the past few years, most of the critical intellectuals have been forced to leave the countries, among them prominent scientists, journalists and academics. Although there is no universally accepted definition of academic freedom, UNESCO defines it "as freedom of teaching and discussion; freedom in carrying out research and disseminating and publishing the results thereof; freedom to express freely their opinion about the institution or system in which they work; freedom from institutional censorship; freedom to participate in professional or representative academic bodies" (UNESCO, 1997). Thus, academics should have the right to pursue, advance, create and disseminate knowledge through research, not only inside, but outside of academia as well. UNESCO's definition above implies that scholars should have the freedom to conduct research, teach or communicate ideas or facts without being targeted for job loss, suppression, prosecution or imprisonment. "Our model for academic freedom", Edward Said wrote, "should be the migrant or traveller […]. The traveller crosses over, traverses' territory, and abandons fixed positions, all the time" (Said, 2000, 404).

There have been a few headline-grabbing cases of repression of academic freedom in Central Asia. These include the case of Alexander Sodiqov, a Tajikistani citizen studying at the University of Toronto, who was arrested on charges of espionage when conducting research in Khorog, Tajikistan, on behalf of an international team in 2014. He was detained for three months before international pressure and diplomatic efforts secured his release (Clibbon, 2014). In a wave of repression in Kyrgyzstan in April 2021, political scientist Marat Kazakpayev was arrested on treason charges, with no full details of the accusations released (CESS, 2021). He died in prison 14 months later. PhD candidate Gulzat Alieva was arrested for inciting religious discord for a Facebook post supporting Tengrism. She was acquitted in November 2022. But these extreme examples are the tip of the iceberg of more everyday forms of repression that shape the contours of knowledge production by local scholars. I have been victim of these forms of repression.

In the mid-2010s, I worked as a senior researcher at the Academy of Sciences. While working at this institute, I came under extreme pressure from the government because of the nature of my work. My research on modern history and on the ongoing political slide of the country towards authoritarianism caused irritation and discontent among the authorities. At one of my meetings with them, an employee of the security services told me in a direct context that "I am the most unreliable citizen of my country and an employee of the Academy of Sciences, who has no right to work in this institution". I was subjected to round-the-clock surveillance; my phone was bugged, my online activities monitored and my life at home and work was tracked via "horizontal surveillance" by my colleagues, the *mahalla* (community) committee and other informants. In addition, the authorities organised a special examination of my research work. They wanted to accuse me of "slandering the authorities and damaging the country's image" and undermining the stability of the constitutional system as a dangerous element of society. For security reasons, I was forced to postpone publication and censor my research, which clearly contradicted the official narratives on modern history and government policy. Self-censorship is one of many survival strategies that local scholars use in Central Asia (Janenova, 2019; Sharshenova, in this volume).

In contrast to foreign scholars, for native scholars it is not only their lives, intellectual and academic freedom that is at stake; the safety of their family is also under serious threat. Once, the security service representative in the department told me "today, your eldest son received a good grade in mathematics at school. Your youngest son will not be in kindergarten when you go to pick him up, and we can dismiss your spouse in disgrace. Neither of you will be able to find a job in any higher educational institution or company". While these remained threats, as a result of this pressure, I opted to leave my country together with my sons and my wife. Even after leaving the country, the remaining part of my family at home is still at risk. This is one of the many reasons why I use a pen name to publish and why I cannot return to my homeland, or even some neighbouring states due to fears of being targeted there via transnational repression (see CAPE, 2018; Furstenberg et al., 2021). Thus, the repression of local academics does not end with the departure from the field and home. It continues in the form of transnational repression. For example, scholars who take part in conferences outside of the country are monitored by state organs. Their presentations are recorded, either by a representative of the embassy in that country or by another participant in the conference who acts as an informant. The latter happened to me at a closed workshop in Germany. No public recording of the event was made and the workshop was not attended by any guests. Yet, when I returned home, my director knew everything I had presented, likely hearing it from a compatriot who was also in attendance. On another occasion, I was told to attend an event on corruption in a neighbouring country and record the proceedings myself. While I refused to collaborate with my authorities, this transnational repression not only continues to affect my ability to conduct research and travel to the region, it also leads me to carefully choose the topics I can present in public and inhibits my ability to become a recognised authority on my subject. It is for this reason that some local scholars see themselves forced to work with the local 'organs' to a certain extent, as the following section shows.

Coaptating Academics

Central Asian academics do not only face repression; the organs also try to tempt them into supporting the regime. Half a year after the meeting with my director in which I was accused of espionage, my boss made another attempt to co-opt me. He eagerly asked me to head a group within the so-called "troll factory" and track foreign scientists who criticise the authorities in their articles. Although I would officially become an employee of the security services, this would not be made public. I would be expected to denigrate the opposition and write puff pieces about the regime. Each week, the security services would send a list of topics that I should write about in the coming week. They ordered me to praise the government and criticise the opposition, writing in English, Russian and the local language. For my services to the regime, they offered me 10 GB of paid Internet and the chance to work from home.

My boss promised that this would allow me to eventually become the head of one of the departments at the Academy of Sciences or the dean of the faculty of a university. I thanked him for such a generous offer. When I asked why the government was so interested in what foreign researchers write about the country, my boss said it was none of my business but said that these foreign researchers would not be granted visas and that it was the duty of a patriotic Central Asian scholar to refute their lies.

Local scholars' collaboration with the security services is common for various reasons. They collaborate out of fear of reprisals against them and their families. Some genuinely believe the government narratives. Others are simply seeking to gain a promotion along with the prestige and financial benefits that this entails. One investigation identified at least five people working in the structures of the Ministry of Education who also worked at a "troll factory", creating fake accounts on social networks and bombarding various sites with comments. Tasks included creating positive threads about the government and trolling opponents. The investigation estimated that at least 400 people work at the troll factory.[2]

Many academics are part of the factory without actively contributing. In my case, my name was added to articles drafted by the security services that denigrated the opposition and praised the president. When they were published, I messaged my contacts in the opposition to dissociate myself from these slanderous posts. They responded with understanding and compassion.

Even some of my students were recruited as informants by the security services and reported on my teaching. These students are part of pro-government youth movements with close ties to law enforcement who denounce teachers and their classmates as a way of gaining favours. These students expect special treatment and are exempt from taking exams. Immediately after graduation, these students are promised jobs in the Ministry of Internal Affairs or security services. These youth movements organised lectures during my classes on topics related to patriotism and against extremism. A representative of their group would come to my class and write down the names of the students who did not attend the above-mentioned lectures.

Local students and scholars are not only recruited to spy on each other, but also on foreign researchers. For example, they are frequently recruited to draft reports about local conferences. Such reports emerged from the June 2022 Central Eurasian Studies Society conference in Tashkent, where local scholars and students at the University of World Economy and Diplomacy reported on the presentations of local

---

[2] Citing the investigation would reveal the country in which I lived and so I have elected to not cite the investigation here.

and international experts.³ I know this happens because I was invited to do this myself. Moreover, when I returned from international conferences outside of my country, I was questioned about specific interactions and things that I said. Such surveillance inhibits local scholars' ability to express themselves and leads to self-censorship even when participating in conferences overseas. As such, state surveillance not only harms but also silences Central Asian voices.

Collaboration with Foreigners

Since 2006, I have collaborated with fellow researchers from Europe, the USA, Canada, Japan and Australia. Because of this, I was systematically persecuted by the security organs who viewed my interaction with foreign researchers with particular suspicion. One morning, an academic from Europe arrived at my institute. None of the directors was present and so the academic came and spoke with me. He stated that he wanted to establish cooperation with our department/institute. We had a brief conversation and I told him he would need to speak to my seniors.

Despite this brief interaction, the security services point of contact in my department invited me to his office. He grilled me about the interaction. Did I know this scientist before this meeting at the institute? Was I in contact with him by email before the arrival of this scientist? Maybe one of my European colleagues, familiar researchers, gave my contacts to this scientist? He hinted that I was suspected of collaborating, betraying and transferring secret state information to a representative of a foreign state. I answered that I had never met the man before. The representative changed his tone and suggested that the next time I invite any foreign scientist to a teahouse or restaurant for lunch, in order to get to know each other better and learn more "about the purpose of the visit, about the scientist's research, what he writes what he thinks about the authorities, what cities and regions he plans to go to, whom he will meet". The curator added that all expenses for lunch or dinner would be paid for by the secret services.

The security services in the Central Asian governments are particularly concerned about foreign researchers. The committee on national security in my country has an office that is tasked with monitoring the publications of foreign researchers and compiling reports on their activities. As Lottholz says, "everything we [foreign scholars] write will be seen by governments and may be followed up on" (Lottholz, 2018, 5). Foreign scholars are viewed as agents of foreign states who are seeking to foment instability and cause "coloured revolutions", as was typified by the case of Alex Sodiqov described earlier. Collaborating with foreign scholars, then, as my above example shows, can entail certain risks.

Central Asian researchers need to carefully navigate these risks. When organising interviews or meeting with foreign researchers, they should do so in public

---

³ Under these circumstances, it comes as no surprise that all panels discussing Uzbekistan's politics were cancelled short notice.

places to avoid unnecessary suspicion by the organs of being a spy. Moreover, local scholars should consider the consequences of being seen publicly with a foreign researcher or member of a group that has been labelled a threat and evaluate whether a physical meeting is necessary. Foreign scholars also need to be cognizant of these risks and modify their behaviour by less aggressively pursuing collaborations and being cautious about what information they divulge about their activities to the local researcher. Such practices can reduce the dangers that local scholars face.

Conclusions and Recommendations

As I have tried to show in this essay, researchers from Central Asia face a number of dilemmas related to authoritarian suppression that their privileged foreign colleagues do not suffer from. They cannot simply catch a flight out of the country and move on to a different region if they face pressure from the local authorities. Their lives are intertwined with their research, with greater difficulties separating the "field" from home (Kudaibergenova, 2019). Their citizenship, financial precarity and family connections make them particularly susceptible to government pressure or accusations of espionage. Faced with such threats, many academics opt to actively support the regime or understandably self-censor. Others, like me, are forced to leave their country and publish under pseudonyms, managing to disseminate their research, but undermining their ability to build a public reputation for their expertise. Some chose to exit the country, moving to freer countries where they can better exercise their voice. But with that choice comes the weakening of ties with family at home. In short, no choice comes without sacrifice and risk, both of which are qualitatively different from those borne by foreign colleagues.

There are a number of practical steps that local researchers can take to navigate these threats to their security. These should be incorporated into graduate-level education in the region via programs by external donors. First, scholars in Central Asia need to increase their digital literacy. For example, they should only access professional email accounts via secure platforms such as Proton Mail or Signal. These can be used for sensitive emails. As the security services monitors mobile phones as well, they should try to obtain a phone number/SIM card that is unregistered or registered under a fake name. Similar to foreign researchers working on and in the region (Dall'Agnola, 2023), local scholars need to pay greater attention to the physical security of their digital research tools. They should not leave their laptop, Dictaphone or camera at their apartment or hotel where they can be accessed and stolen by security services.

Finally, foreign researcher organisations such as the Central Eurasian Studies Society should provide training to members on research safety, as well as set up a rapid response task force to respond to emergency situations facing local academics, such as the arrest of Alexander Sodiqov. By taking these measures, the scholarly community can demonstrate solidarity and take practical steps to ensure that the safety of every scholar, whether local or non-local, comes before knowledge creation.

Acknowledgements I would like to thank my family and my international colleagues for their generosity and support as I have navigated these challenges. Naming them would reveal my identity, but I would like to thank them, nonetheless.

References

Bekmurzaev, N., Lottholz, P., & Meyer, J. (2018). Navigating the safety implications of doing research and being researched in Kyrgyzstan: Cooperation, networks and framing. *Central Asian Survey, 37*(1), 100–118. https://doi.org/10.1080/02634937.2017.1419165

CAPE. (2018). *Central Asia political exiles database.* Available at https://excas.net/wp-content/uploads/2020/09/CAPE_Codebook.pdf. Last accessed 19 May 19 2023.

CESS. (2021). *CESS statement on academic freedom in Kyrgyzstan.* Available at https://www.centraleurasia.org/2021/cess-statement-on-academic-freedom-in-kyrgyzstan/. Last accessed 19 May 2023.

Clibbon, J. (2014, September 13). How Alexander Sodiqov was freed following espionage charges. *CBC.* https://www.cbc.ca/news/world/how-alexander-sodiqov-was-freedfollowing-espionage-charges-1.2772191

Dall'Agnola, J. (2023). Fieldwork under surveillance: A research note. *Surveillance & Society 21*(2). https://doi.org/10.24908/ss.v21i2.16455

Furstenberg, S., Lemon, E., & Heathershaw, J. (2021). Spatialising state practices through transnational repression. *European Journal of International Security, 6*(3), 358–378. https://doi.org/10.1017/eis.2021.10

Gentile, M. (2013). Meeting the 'organs': The tacit dilemma of field research in authoritarian states. *Area, 45*(4), 426–432. https://doi.org/10.1111/area.12030

Glasius, M., de Lange, M., Bartman, J., Dalmasso, E., Ly, A., Del Sordi, A., Michaelsen, M., & Ruijgork, K. (2018). *Research, ethics and risk in the authoritarian field.* Palgrave Macmillan.

Hirschman, A. (1970). *Exit, voice, and loyalty.* Harvard University Press.

Janenova, S. (2019). The boundaries of research in an authoritarian state. *International Journal of Qualitative Methods, 18*, 1–8. https://doi.org/10.1177/1609406919876469

Kinzelbach et al. (2023). *Academic freedom index.* Available at https://policycommons.net/artifacts/3456334/afi-update-2022/4256707/. Last accessed 19 May 2023.

Koch, N. (2013). Introduction—Field methods in 'closed contexts': Undertaking research in authoritarian states and places. *Area, 45*(4), 390–395. https://doi.org/10.1111/area.12044

Kudaibergenova, D. (2019, October 7). When your field is also your home: Introducing feminist subjectivities in Central Asia. *openDemocracy.* https://www.opendemocracy.net/en/odr/when-your-field-also-your-home-ntroducingfeminist-subjectivities-central-asia/

Lottholz, P. (2018). Researcher safety in peace, conflict and security studies in Central Asia and beyond: Making sense and finding new ways forward. *Security Praxis*: 1–7.

Perry, E. (2020). Educated acquiescence: How academia sustains authoritarianism in China. *Theory & Society, 49*(5), 1–22. https://doi.org/10.1007/s11186-019-09373-1

Roche, S. (2018). The fabric of answer: Constructing a national facade. *Central Asian Affairs, 5*(2), 93–110. https://doi.org/10.1163/22142290-00502001

Said, E. (2000). *Out of place: A memoir.* Vintage.

Sharshenova, A. Safety, security, and self-censorship as survival strategies. In: Dall'Agnola, J & Sharshenova, A (Eds), *SpringerBriefs in Political Science.* Researching Central Asia.

Sökefeld, M., & Strasser, S. (2016). Introduction: under suspicious eyes—Surveillance states, security zones and ethnographic fieldwork. *Zeitschrift Für Ethnologie, 141*(2), 159–176.

Trevisani, T. (2016). Under suspicious eyes: Work and fieldwork in a steel plant in Kazakhstan. *Zeitschrift Für Ethnologie, 141*(2), 281–297.

UNESCO. (1997). *Status of higher-education teaching personnel (recommendation)*. Available at https://en.unesco.org/about-us/legal-affairs/recommendation-concerning-status-higher-education-teaching-personnel. Last accessed 23 May 2023.

Ruslan Norov is the penname of a researcher from Central Asia. Due to the threats made against him, some of which are outlined in his chapter for this book, he has elected to remain anonymous. He is now based in Europe and continues to conduct research on political issues in the region.

Open Access This chapter is licensed under the terms of the Creative Commons Attribution 4.0 International License (http://creativecommons.org/licenses/by/4.0/), which permits use, sharing, adaptation, distribution and reproduction in any medium or format, as long as you give appropriate credit to the original author(s) and the source, provide a link to the Creative Commons license and indicate if changes were made.

The images or other third party material in this chapter are included in the chapter's Creative Commons license, unless indicated otherwise in a credit line to the material. If material is not included in the chapter's Creative Commons license and your intended use is not permitted by statutory regulation or exceeds the permitted use, you will need to obtain permission directly from the copyright holder.

Chapter 10
Performative Heterosexuality: A Gay Researcher Doing Fieldwork in Central Asia

Marius Honig

Abstract This chapter explores the challenges faced by a foreign gay researcher in Central Asia. Drawing on personal experiences, the author reflects on the limited choices available to LGBTQ+ researchers to protect themselves, the practicalities and consequences of hiding one's sexuality, and the limitations of performing a heterosexual male identity in the field. The author explains the strategies employed to protect their safety and the ethical consequences of silencing their own identity and values. The author also emphasises how choices made by researchers studying Central Asia become permanent features of their professional life due to long-lasting involvement in the region.

Keywords Positionality · LGBTQ+ · Masculinity · Fieldwork · Safety

Introduction

The situation of LGBTQ+ rights in Central Asia is troubling and "social stigma, homophobia, and harassment are widespread" (Talant, 2022). Caravanistan, a popular tourist guide for travels along the Silk Roads reports that "stories of homosexuals being beaten, raped (if a woman) or ultimately murdered are depressingly common" and that "you would not want to be too open about your sexual orientation anywhere [in the region]" (2019). In two out of five Central Asian countries, Uzbekistan and Turkmenistan, male homosexuality is even punishable by law (Dall'Agnola, 2023b). It is in this context that my experience as a gay researcher doing fieldwork in Central Asia took place. When confronted with the question of personal safety, I decided to hide my sexuality to protect my safety in the field, a common choice for LGBTQ+ researchers (Hughes, 2018; Ragen, 2017). The challenges that my choice produced and the consequences arising from it are the topic of this article.

M. Honig (✉)
Iserlohn, Germany

© The Author(s) 2024
J. Dall'Agnola and A. Sharshenova (eds.), *Researching Central Asia*,
SpringerBriefs in Political Science,
https://doi.org/10.1007/978-3-031-39024-1_10

Recent research in queer studies has focused on sexuality and membership in the LGBTQ+ community in discussing the intersectional challenges in social research (Browne & Nash, 2016; Heil, 2021; Stenson, 2022). However, it is far less common to discuss the challenges faced by LGBTQ+ researchers outside queer studies (Zebracki & Greatrick, 2022). In the field of post-Soviet studies, many women researchers, some of whom are part of the LGBTQ+ community (Kamarauskaitė, 2023), have researched the position of a woman doing fieldwork in Eurasia, however, there is no research that combines area studies with a discussion on the positionality of a gay man, particularly in Central Asia.

After collocating my journey in the literature, I will use some anonymised stories from my fieldwork to discuss my positionality as a gay foreign researcher who is hiding his identity. My reflections expose the consequences of my performative heterosexuality in the Central Asian context, as well as the effect of applying a preconceived idea of masculinity in Central Asia in limiting the space for the expression of personal ideas and values, therefore empowering heteronormative behaviours. I will also discuss the limited choices that an LGBTQ+ researcher is confronted with and the effects of the compromises we need to accept. Finally, I will underline how alternative choices could have been possible, particularly given that the status of Central Asian studies makes some of these choices a permanent feature of my professional life.

Performing Heterosexuality During Fieldwork

I agree with Zebracki and Greatrick's (2022) critique that the distinction between being inside and outside the field for members of the LGBTQ+ community is not clearcut. In the context of Central Asia, the researcher-respondent relationship is even more complex. The status of "area expert" muddles the distinction between being inside and outside the field, where the entrance in the field is clearcut, but the exit disappears. The field involves the entire professional life of a researcher and does not necessarily stop when the fieldwork ends.

Feminist scholars have described gender as performative and socially constructed (Butler, 1990; Cupples, 2002). Some important research has been dedicated in Central Asian studies to female researchers and the influence of being a woman doing fieldwork in Central Asia (Thibault, 2021; Turlubekova, 2023). Taking from this precious work, I turn to discuss the challenges of performing the role of a heterosexual man to hide my LGBTQ+ identity, resting on the concept of performative male gender. When discussing the importance of sex and sexuality in fieldwork settings, Cupples (2002, 383) writes that "when we go into the field, we often go as members of a group of people of which our researched community already has a preconceived image". This means that going into the field as a Western heterosexual man will not only create expectations about my race and nationality, around for example liberal values, but also about my masculinity, which will in turn be influenced by culturally specific ideas of what it means to be a man in Central Asia. At the same time, attempts at being "culturally sensitive" mean that male foreign researchers might decide to stress or hide aspects of their identity depending on their preconceived idea of what is expected from them in the cultural context (Cupples, 2002; Linneken in Flinn et al., 1998).

The hegemonic status of heterosexuality influences the expectations around what it means to be a proper man, or woman, in a heteronormative sense. Jackson (2006) provides a complete account of the normative aspects of heterosexuality as a complete social act. According to him, being a heterosexual man does not only imply having sex with women, but also a full set of behaviours that make a specific and culturally connotated heterosexual man. The use of "heterosexual normative behaviour" to construct an idea of a traditional man is very common, and is a known phenomenon in the post-Soviet space (Kudaibergenova, 2019). My act in the field can be considered performative heterosexuality, but this conceptualisation of heteronormativity implies that mine might not have been the only performance. When leaving the public space, however, the role of my homosexuality as a hidden identity has formed part of my experience of the field. In this discussion, I take from the literature on clashes of values and other personal circumstances between researchers' and their participants or assistants (Dall'Agnola, 2023a).

All the reflections above on being a male LGBTQ+ Western scholar in the discipline of Central Asia studies rest on the assumption that the "stance or positioning of the researcher in relation to the social and political concept of the study" and "the researcher's insider or outsider relationship to the community engaged with the enquiry" (Coghlan & Brydon-Miller, 2014, 1) influences their research. The insider/outsider aspect of my positionality is a central aspect of this research in that, by hiding my real position as a gay man for my personal safety, I played with the boundaries of privilege and reduced the intersectional challenges that can impact fieldwork research. Intersectionality is defined here as "the assertion that social identity categories such as race, gender, class, sexuality, and ability are interconnected and operate simultaneously to produce experiences of both privilege and marginalisation" (Smooth, 2013, 11). However, as expressed above, the personal and private side of my choices entails the alienation of a real personal connection with the field, the choice of research over personal connections. These theoretical reflections will be explored through a number of model situations that I will modify sufficiently to prevent recognition by anyone involved while retaining enough to maintain their reflective purpose.

Hiding in Plain Sight

During the process of attaining ethical approval at my university, I soon noticed that no guidance was available for LGBTQ+ researchers on protecting their own safety during fieldwork, and that much of the literature was related to LGBTQ+ researchers doing research on queer communities, and thus often focussed on respondents more than researchers (Anonymous, 2021; Dodd, 2013; Heil, 2021). Through my funding body, I was put in contact with a network of LGBTQ+ researchers, which was in the process of producing a handbook for LGBTQ+ researchers doing research in difficult contexts, and to which I have contributed (Zebracki & Greatrick, forthcoming). Through engagement with this community, I was finally able to design a strategy for my fieldwork.

The first step of my strategy was to polish my online presence by removing any reference to my sexuality from social media, something which has now become a permanent choice due to my professional connection with Central Asia. This resulted in my political engagement in the LGBTQ+ community being relegated to the personal sphere in an act of self-censorship (Ho, 2008). The second aspect of my online strategy was to protect my personal information through the use of security apps, such as Virtual Private Networks (VPNs), password managers and constant vigilance on my profiles. In one case, I received a suspicious public comment under a post on one of my social media profiles referring to the treatment of homosexuality in the place where I was about to do fieldwork. While I have no proof that the person who wrote it was aware of my sexuality, this episode imposed a reflection on the potential danger of cybersurveillance of researchers' online presence, and the impacts of this on physical and mental safety, particularly in the case of LGBTQ+ researchers.

In the offline realm, my decision was to be as open as possible with local authorities in terms of what my research was about. This is not the preferred choice for many researchers as it implies a scrutiny of one's research project, as well as a connection with local institutions, often expressions of the local government. In my case, this choice arose from the strategy of "hiding in plain sight", where public engagement with local authorities functioned as a safeguard for my own personal safety. This, in turn, played with my insider/outsider perspective, giving me privileged institutional access with which to conduct my research.

Moving to the personal consequences of my safety strategy, getting back into the closet had an important effect on my perspective on the fieldwork. In particular, the personal connections that I have built throughout my time in the region, although very developed in some cases, were based on a partial sharing of my own identity. At the same time, however, a partial polishing of LGBTQ+ identity is perfectly common in European societies. According to Greatrick (2021), members of the LGBTQ+ community have been trained all their lives to hide and are, therefore, uniquely equipped to be able to assess the extent of compromises they are going to accept in the context of fieldwork. It is, therefore, important to note that my personal experience is based on specific choices that were not imposed on me by any institutions, nor should they have been. This implies consequently that other choices could have been made. One night when I was in the field, a friend who was and still is not aware of my sexuality invited me to a performance. When I sat down to a two-hour narration of an LGBTQ+ story, I was hit by a mix of amazement, fear and admiration. LGBTQ+ communities and people exist everywhere, and my choice to go back to the closet removed the agency of my local contacts to accept my sexuality and engage positively with my identity (Sou, 2021).

Comradery and Rituality in Central Asia

While I made sure never to directly lie to anyone about myself, I have misled my contacts to assume that I was a heterosexual man. In the society that I found myself in, women and men tend to socialise in separated groups. Hence, the core of my social activities happened among men. Some of these contexts involved discussions about women that assumed everyone in the room was attracted to women. Every time I engaged with a woman in professional terms together with a male colleague, comments on their physical appearance would follow that put me in the position of having to reply to direct questions on women's appearance. During meals, the flirting with women colleagues, usually Central Asian, would be relentless, while I would receive gazes from male colleagues looking for a comrade, an insider, with whom to share appreciation for women. While I would never accept such behaviour in my home University, I found myself neutrally commenting on women's physical appearances, as well as responding to men winking at me about their female colleagues. The performative character of my heterosexuality led me to assume that, if I refused to comment on women's appearance, as I am sure many heterosexual colleagues do, I could have endangered my performance.

However, in more in-depth discussion where the level of proximity and comradery was higher, the space for discussions also got larger. For example, when on one occasion, one of my comrades argued that Central Asian women differ from women in Europe in their desire for gender equality and rights, I felt safe enough to disagree. However, even in that situation, I was very careful to refer to men and women in the context of heterosexual relationships and to not talk about my own experience in relationships with women as a gay man. As such, I was stressing the similarities between heteronormative behaviours in Europe and Central Asia without allowing for alternative discussions to permeate our conversations. In playing the role of a liberal Western man, I limited the discussion between my respondents and myself to the heteronormative context. However, through these compromises, I was actually silencing them and myself, avoiding some specific topics of conversation. In short, by performing my role as a heterosexual man, I created obstacles and allowed for those performative behaviours to prevent real/deep connections from forming between my interlocutors and myself.

Another aspect of my heteronormative performance involved my physical interpretation of manhood in Central Asia. I usually wear a long beard, which in Central Asia is perceived as a symbol of religiosity. I discussed this issue with Central Asian colleagues before going to the region and I was advised to cut my beard shorter. Furthermore, the formality of the academic sector in the destination of my fieldwork made it easier for me to disguise my queerness in a smart suit. However, for as much as I was trying to adopt the Central Asian physical appearance of a (heterosexual) man, I was still perceived as a Western man and judged accordingly. While the choice of cutting my beard as well as being overly formal was not fundamental, other expectations of Western men became more central. For example, the habit of drinking alcohol among male colleagues.

Even if Central Asian society is for the majority Muslim, attitudes towards drinking alcohol remain very liberal (Ro'i & Wainer, 2009). This is particularly true at the elite level, with celebratory meals involving several shots of vodka. My sobriety was met with surprise and some disappointment in the region. Drinking has an important role in post-Soviet societies and the decision not to drink comes with consequences in terms of comradery (Hervouet, 2019). In my own story, the decision to quit drinking was to avoid loss of inhibition and control. While alcohol is routinely used by researchers in the post-Soviet space to create rapport (see Hervouet, 2019 and Driscoll, 2015, footnote 38 on page 21 for a good narration), my peculiar position as performative heterosexual stopped me from doing so, as drinking could have revealed sides of myself that I had decided to hide. My decision is also connected with ethical issues arising from the use of alcohol by white men doing research in the Global South, such as power differentials or the effects of alcohol on judgement, as well as the social implications of drinking in terms of gender, class and race (Gillen, 2015). However, renouncing the drinking culture of Central Asian elites surely impacted the depth of connections that I made in the region and any future links that I could use for my career. These career-related obstacles are part of the many aspects of inequality that LGBTQ+ , female and BAME researchers face on a daily basis.

Conclusion

As I have tried to show in this essay, the compromises and contradictions of being an LGBTQ+ researcher in a Central Asian context where LGBTQ+ rights are restricted by law are rarely discussed in written form. While reflecting on my chosen safety strategy before, in and after my fieldwork in Central Asia, I expose the lack of preparation on the side of my university in guiding me in the process of building an ethical strategy and highlight the importance of peer-to-peer networks of support for LGBTQ+ researchers doing fieldwork. I also stress the fact that none of my choices were inevitable and that many of the safety measures I chose to apply to my fieldwork arose from compromises and choices that felt right in my own case, and thus should not be used as a model. My choices will have consequences that go beyond the fieldwork. As an area studies scholar, my engagement with the field did not stop after going back to Europe. Therefore, many of my strategies have become permanent features of my professional life.

At the same time, my decision to hide my identity has removed agency from the Central Asian people I engaged with to interact with my real identity. Sou (2021) writes how the choice of hiding one's own identity withdraws any possibility of people in the fieldwork destination engaging with one's sexuality and contributes to silencing them. I would add that, in the personal sphere, hiding my homosexuality from my peers has made it impossible for my local friends to know me for real. My public position in the field was that of a heterosexual man, which opened the door to a number of privileges, such as access to situations of heterosexual comradery, for me.

At the same time, I performed a heteronormative version of a foreign heterosexual man. While the appearance, behaviour and political ideas of a European heterosexual man are given much larger room to manoeuvre in the Central Asian context, my performative identity restricted my perception of this room and led me to use it only where the conversations happened in a private space.

The choices that LGBTQ+ researchers are forced to make, although contestable, need to be taken into account when discussing inclusivity policies in academic spaces and the ethical considerations of fieldwork research. The effects of being a member of the LGBTQ+ community on researchers' lives and careers, such as renouncing a publication by writing under a pen name, should function as a reminder of the obstacles that our community faces inside and outside the field.

References

Anonymous. (2021, May 4). Back in 'the closet': Conducting fieldwork as an LGBTQ+ researcher. Pride in the field. *Geography Directions*. https://blog.geographydirections.com/2021/05/04/back-in-the-closet-conducting-fieldwork-as-an-lgbtq-researcher/

Browne, K., & Nash, C. (2016). Queer Methods and Methodologies: An introduction. In K. Browne & C. Nash (Eds.), *Queer methods and methodologies: Intersecting queer theories and social science research*. Taylor & Francis. https://doi.org/10.4324/9781315603223

Butler, J. (1990). *Gender trouble: Feminism and the subversion of identity*. Routledge.

Caravanistan. (2019). *Silk road travel for LGBT*. https://caravanistan.com/planning/lgbt/

Coghlan, D., & Brydon-Miller, M. (2014). *The SAGE encyclopedia of action research*. SAGE Publications Ltd. https://doi.org/10.4135/9781446294406

Cupples, J. (2002). The field as a landscape of desire: Sex and sexuality in geographical fieldwork. *Area, 34*(4), 382–390. https://doi.org/10.1111/1475-4762.00095

Dall'Agnola, J. (2023a). The challenges of fieldwork in post-soviet societies. In J. Dall'Agnola, A. Edwards, & M. Howlett (Eds.), *Researching in the former Soviet Union. Stories from the field*. BASEES/Routledge Series. https://doi.org/10.4324/9781003144168-1

Dall'Agnola, J. (2023b). Smartphones and public support for LGBTQ+ in Central Asia. *Central Asian Survey*. https://doi.org/10.1080/02634937.2023.2187346

Dodd, S. (2013). LGBTQ: Protecting vulnerable subjects in all studies. In D. Mertens & P. Ginsberg (Eds.), *The handbook of social research ethics* (pp. 474–488). SAGE.

Driscoll, J. (2015). *Warlords and coalition politics in post-Soviet States*. Cambridge University Press. https://doi.org/10.1017/CBO9781107478046

Flinn, J., Marshall, L., & Armstrong, J. (1998). *Fieldwork and families: Constructing new models for ethnographic research*. University of Hawai'i Press.

Gillen, J. (2015). Rethinking whiteness and masculinity in geography: Drinking alcohol in the field in Vietnam. *Antipode, 48*, 584–602. https://doi.org/10.1111/anti.12202

Greatrick, A. (2021, February 9). LGBTQ+ inclusive fieldwork. Pride in the field. *Geography Directions*. https://blog.geographydirections.com/2022/06/09/lgbtq-inclusive-fieldwork-repost/

Heil, T. (2021). Muslim–Queer encounters in Rio de Janeiro: Making sense of relational positionalities. *Ethnography, 22*(1), 31–50. https://doi.org/10.1177/1466138119859601

Hervouet, R. (2019). A political ethnography of rural communities under an authoritarian regime: The case of Belarus. *Bulletin of Sociological Methodology/Bulletin De Méthodologie Sociologique, 141*(1), 85–112. https://doi.org/10.1177/0759106318812790

Ho, E. (2008). Embodying self-censorship: Studying, writing and communicating. *Area, 40*(4), 491–499. https://doi.org/10.1111/j.1475-4762.2008.00821.x

Hughes, C. (2018). Not out in the field: Studying privacy and disclosure as an invisible (Trans) man. In D. Compton, T. Meadow, & K. Schilt (Eds.), *Other please specify: Queer methods in sociology* (pp. 111–125). University of California Press.

Jackson, S. (2006). Gender, sexuality and heterosexuality: The complexity (and limits) of heteronormativity. *Feminist Theory, 7*(1), 105–121. https://doi.org/10.1177/1464700106061462

Kamarauskaité, R. (2023). Doing fieldwork (not quite) at home: Reflecting on an expat's positionality in Lithuania. In J. Dall'Agnola, A. Edwards, & M. Howlett (Eds.), *Researching in the former Soviet Union* (pp. 53–70). BASEES/Routledge Series. https://doi.org/10.4324/9781003144168-5

Kudaibergenova, D. T. (2019). The body global and the body traditional: A digital ethnography of instagram and nationalism in Kazakhstan and Russia. *Central Asian Survey, 38*(3), 363–380. https://doi.org/10.1080/02634937.2019.1650718

Ragen, B. (2017, June 28). Being Queer in the jungle: The unique challenges of LGBTQ scientists working in the field. *Research in Progress Blog.* https://blogs.biomedcentral.com/bmcblog/2017/06/28/being-queer-in-the-jungle-the-unique-challenges-of-lgbtq-scientists-working-in-the-field/

Ro'i, Y., & Wainer, A. (2009). Muslim identity and Islamic practice in post-soviet Central Asia. *Central Asian Survey, 28*(3), 303–322. https://doi.org/10.1080/02634930903421863

Smooth, W. (2013). Intersectionality from theoretical framework to policy intervention. *Situating Intersectionality: Politics, Policy, and Power, 11–41.* https://doi.org/10.1057/9781137025135_2

Sou, G. (2021). Concealing researcher identity in fieldwork and social media: Sexuality and speaking for participants. *Area, 53*, 473–480. https://doi.org/10.1111/area.12736

Stenson, A. (2022). Queer positionality and researching University lad culture. *Social Sciences, 11*(12). https://doi.org/10.3390/socsci11120562

Talant, B. (2022, June 10). Life as an LGBT person in Central Asia. *Radio Free Europe/Radio Liberty.* https://www.rferl.org/a/life-as-an-lgbtq-person-central-asia/31892168.html

Thibault, H. (2021). 'Are you married?': Gender and faith in political ethnographic research. *Journal of Contemporary Ethnography, 50*(3), 395–416. https://doi.org/10.1177/0891241620986852

Turlubekova, Z. (2023). A woman of her word prepared for the worst. Researching drug trafficking in Kazakhstan. In J. Dall'Agnola, A. Edwards, & M. Howlett (Eds.), *Researching in the former Soviet Union* (pp. 53–70). BASEES/Routledge Series. https://doi.org/10.4324/9781003144168-5

Zebracki, M., & Greatrick, A. (2022). Inclusive LGBTQ+ fieldwork: Advancing spaces of belonging and safety. *Area, 54*(4), 551–557. https://doi.org/10.1111/area.12828

Zebracki, M., & Greatrick, A. (forthcoming). *Handbook of LGBTQ+ inclusive fieldwork.* Available at SSRN: https://ssrn.com/abstract=3969874

Marius Honig is a pseudonym, a German translation of the name of the Italian revolutionary queer theorist Mario Mieli. Reading the abstract, it is easy to understand why the author decided to cover up their identity. It suffices to say that the country where the researcher was doing fieldwork is a dangerous place for LGBTQ+ people. The only relevant detail about the researcher that will be shared are that they are from a Western country, they are white, and they are in their 30s and doing research in the social sciences at an early career stage in a European University.

Open Access This chapter is licensed under the terms of the Creative Commons Attribution 4.0 International License (http://creativecommons.org/licenses/by/4.0/), which permits use, sharing, adaptation, distribution and reproduction in any medium or format, as long as you give appropriate credit to the original author(s) and the source, provide a link to the Creative Commons license and indicate if changes were made.

The images or other third party material in this chapter are included in the chapter's Creative Commons license, unless indicated otherwise in a credit line to the material. If material is not included in the chapter's Creative Commons license and your intended use is not permitted by statutory regulation or exceeds the permitted use, you will need to obtain permission directly from the copyright holder.

Chapter 11
From Romantic Advances to Cyberstalking in the Field

Jasmin Dall'Agnola

Abstract So far, the implications of sexual advances and cyberstalking on fieldworkers' personal and professional lives have been rarely discussed in published form. While collecting data for my postdoctoral project in Central Asia, I experienced various forms of sexual harassment, ranging from unwelcomed sexual verbal and physical advances, whistling and catcalling to stalking both off- and online. In being honest and transparent about my personal experiences with unwanted sexual advances in the field, I neither wish to draw generalisations about Central Asian men, nor to discourage other female scholars from conducting fieldwork in the region. By contrast, I hope that my personal reflections will help other researchers mitigate and avoid similar situations.

Keywords Sexual harassment · Cyberstalking · Fieldwork · Central Asia

Introduction

A casually dressed 19-year-old woman boards a coach on the outskirts of a small city. Apart from the driver and two other passengers, the vehicle is empty. The young woman chooses a window seat. At the next stop, three people, including a man in his early sixties, enter. After having bought his ticket, the old man locks eyes with the 19-year-old. With his eyes wide open and licking his lips, the old man's *viol par le*

J. Dall'Agnola (✉)
The George Washington University, Washington, DC, USA
e-mail: jasmin.dallagnola@gwu.edu

regard[1] sends cold chills down her spine. Anxiously the young woman gazes out of the window. The 60-year-old slowly makes his way through the coach and chooses the free seat right next to her. The woman is now trapped between the window and the old man. Still glancing at her, the 60-year-old tries to make a move on the 19-year-old. Shocked by his inappropriate behaviour, the woman pretends that she does not speak the local vernacular and ignores him. This does not prevent the old man from moving closer to the young woman and putting his hand on her knee. Realising that no one will help her, the 19-year-old looks at the old man and says in Russian: "What do you want from me? I do not understand you!" Not knowing Russian, the old man points at himself and says: "I am Peter" and then points at the young woman "and you?" "Elena" answers the woman. Peter removes his hand from her knee and takes her hand instead. "Are you married to a local man?" "Boyfriend" Elena replies in a broken English. Peter releases her hand and jokingly reprimands her that she needs to learn the local language to remain in the country. Peter finally ceases his advances. Pointing at herself and the door, Elena tries to explain to Peter that she has to get off at the next stop. He cordially lets her pass. Before leaving the coach, Elena turns around and angrily shouts at Peter in the local language: "You are a f** pervert! And everyone else here", she points at the other passengers, "should feel ashamed for standing by and doing nothing".

Many of my female interlocutors in Central Asia can sympathise with Elena's story. Sexual harassment of teenage girls and women in public transport is pervasive in Central Asian societies. There are no laws criminalising sexual harassment (Abdullaeva, 2021; Dall'Agnola, 2022; Kulakhmetova & Zhailau, 2022) and men's treatment of women in public spaces has not received much attention in the region until very recently. However, upon revealing that I am Elena and that I became the victim of sexual harassment in a small city in the countryside of Switzerland, my female respondents tend to be speechless. I decided to start this essay with my own personal experience of sexual harassment in Switzerland to show that this issue is not a Central Asian problem per se. A study of 4500 Swiss women carried out by the survey institute, GfS Bern for Amnesty International Switzerland in 2019 (Amnesty International Switzerland, 2019), revealed that one in five women has been a victim of sexual violence, and almost 60 per cent had been subjected to sexual harassment in the form of unwanted touching, close physical contact or kissing. I, therefore, do not regard Central Asia as any more dangerous for women than Switzerland; both societies exhibit unacceptably high levels of sexual harassment and violence against women. As such, in contrast to female researchers who experienced few incidents of sexual harassment in their life prior to their fieldwork overseas (Congdon, 2015), I was well aware of the possibility of sexual harassment when embarking on my second field trip to Central Asia in 2022.

While collecting data for my postdoctoral project in the region, I experienced various forms of sexual harassment, ranging from unwelcomed sexual verbal and physical advances, whistling, and catcalling to stalking both off- and online. In

---

[1] A French term for "eye rape" that is used to describe a man's leering stare (eyes wide and mouth hanging open) at a woman for an unnaturally extended period of time.

being honest and transparent about my personal experiences with unwanted sexual advances in the field, I neither wish to make totalising generalisations about Central Asian men, nor to discourage other female scholars from conducting fieldwork in the region. By contrast, I hope that my personal reflections presented here will help other researchers mitigate and avoid similar situations.

The remainder of this essay is organised as follows. In the first section, I show why my foreign femininity attracted much attention from male interlocutors and how I managed to ward off some of the unwanted sexual advances in the field. Then, I discuss how the popularisation of new technologies has transformed the strategies and tools that can be utilised by men to harass women while discussing my own experience with cyberstalking.

Navigating Unwanted Sexual Advances in the Field

When returning to Central Asia to conduct interviews for my postdoctoral project, I knew that it was impossible for me "to maintain a fiction of a genderless self" (Moreno, 1995, 246) vis-a-vis my interlocutors in the field. Indeed, the most significant aspects of my positionality, which determined both female and male respondents' reactions towards me were my youth and white European femininity. While young women, in particular, would use the interview with me as an opportunity to engage in discourses of inclusion and gender equality, most young men in their twenties and thirties would misread my interest in their use of technologies as an attempt to flirt with them. In this context, the well-meant advice from established female researchers to wear an engagement ring turned out to be quite ineffective in my case.

For example, on one evening, a pot-bellied man in his early thirties squeezed himself into the lift with me. Aziz[2] grinned at me. Hoping that I could recruit him for an interview, I smiled back politely. When the lift began moving upwards, he casually asked me if I had any plans for the evening. Caught off guard and flustered, I replied with a no and mentioned that I was looking to interview people for my research. Aziz replied that he was happy to answer all of my questions over dinner. Pointing at my engagement ring, I politely declined. Aziz smiled and argued that my *fiancé* was absent and therefore, would never find out about our rendezvous. Outraged by his indecent proposal, I tried to push past him to leave the lift one floor earlier. As I went by, Aziz leered and stated that if I ever wanted any company, I should just come to his apartment, as he had bought some nice red wine for the occasion.

Many young men like Aziz, made it quite clear what they wanted in return for their participation. Some made physical sexual advances, others were verbally explicit, and yet, others restricted themselves to hints and allusions. So, yes, "I had men's attention" (Thibault, 2021, 13), but this had its price. In contrast to Central Asian

---

[2] To protect the anonymity of my interlocutors, all names used in this account are pseudonyms. For the same reason, I avoid mentioning specific places, cities and countries I visited in Central Asia.

women who were there for serious courtship and marriage, foreign women, like me, were seen as sexually promiscuous and therefore were there "for fun" (Peinhopf, 2023, 28). My meetings with local men were not regulated by local gender behaviour rules. As such, I was neither protected by these norms nor did men feel obliged to respect my personal boundaries. That for some men, I seemed to resemble Maria Sharapova, the Russian tennis star, made the situation no better. Among the more "bearable" unwanted romantic advances were compliments on my looks, explicit flirting, being asked out and inquiries about the whereabouts of my *fiancé*. More unbearable and therefore, more difficult to navigate and ward off were the nightly phone calls, indecent proposals to become someone's second wife, sexualised threats and physical sexual advances by men in power.

The repeated sexual advances from gatekeepers and other men in power proved especially challenging. I needed their support to access the field and my respondents. Outright rejections of their proposals, therefore, could have harmed both my safety and my research. On one occasion, I had to visit a local registration office to secure permission for my stay. On arrival, I was asked by a senior male administrative official to leave my passport with him overnight. I remember feeling anxious and naked without my passport. Yet, this was the only way to obtain the necessary permission for my stay. The following day, I therefore eagerly returned to the office to relocate my documents. I approached the same officer and asked him whether my registration had been done. Holding my passport in his hand, the official stared at me from head to toe. To his seeming despair, I had covered my hair and I was wearing a long wide grey dress. Licking his lips, he insisted on continuing our talk in the back of his office. We could speed up my registration with *trachat* (a vulgar Russian term for "sexual intercourse"). I managed to wriggle out of this situation by playing extremely "dumb", pretending that I did not understand what he wanted and feigning another appointment in the city. Upon returning to my apartment, my self-confident façade crumbled, and I sobbed out of fear and relief that I had gotten my passport back without being raped by a male official. Since, I evidently had little to give in terms of power and wealth, men in power were demanding sexual favours from me in exchange for their help. However, succumbing to the sexual advances of these men was never an option for me.

Two months after the incident at the registration office, I was again forced to keep my opinion to myself to avoid offending one of my main gatekeepers in another city. Akmat kept on calling me at night. He was concerned about my personal safety: "Oh my dear Jasmin, you are a smart girl, but you are also a beautiful girl. So, one of our boys might kidnap you. You know we have this tradition to abduct our women for marriage". Even after explaining to him that I was already engaged to a man in Switzerland, Akmat insisted, "but you know my beloved Jasmin, your father will receive good money for you. Don't you think, he would be happy about this?" Akmat kept on repeating these sexualised threats, even when he introduced me to potential interviewees. He would jokingly introduce me to his friends as "Jasmin, the researcher from Switzerland who soon will be abducted because of her exotic beauty". To remain in his good books, it was only on our last meeting that I summoned the courage to counter him: "Akmat, I know my dear father. He will only accept a bride-price of more than one million USD for me. If any man dares to disrespect my father, well, my father will introduce him to his friends from the mafia". Given my Italian surname, it was clear which mafia I meant. My response had the intended effect. Akmat ceased calling me at night and I never saw him again during my stay in the country. However, some Central Asian men continued their unwanted sexual advances online long after I had left the field, as the following section shows.

Cyber Harassment and Stalking

Upon agreeing to talk with me, my gatekeepers would usually connect me with their friends, colleagues and/or acquaintances on WhatsApp, Instagram or Telegram. While I had some concerns about this practice, sharing personal contact information with strangers is often unavoidable to acquire respondents in any field site. Luckily, apart from one male interviewee, who I had to block after he threatened to turn me into his princess when I returned to his city, none of the Central Asian men with whom I had willingly exchanged my contact details harassed me online.

I did, however, have one encounter with a Central Asian man, Amir, whom I had not given my private phone number to, but who used his personal links to the authorities to obtain it against my will. Amir interrupted my business lunch with a local female academic. He wanted to invite me for dinner in one of the most expensive restaurants in the city. According to him, I reminded him of a French actress he used to admire when he was a young boy. My friend, seemingly intimidated by Amir's presence, whispered that Amir resembled a local politician and therefore, could be an interesting respondent for my study. I gave Amir my business card with the clear message that I was only interested in meeting him for business purposes. We shook hands and parted. Not thinking further about Amir, I went on to other meetings that day. Around nine o'clock in the evening, I checked my phone and noticed that there were several missed calls from an unknown local phone number as well as a message on WhatsApp from the same number. Reading the text, I froze: "Jasmin. Good evening. I am very sorry for calling and texting you without further notice. Amir". I was shocked. How had Amir succeeded in getting my Swiss number? My Swiss phone number was neither printed on my business card nor was it publicly available on social media or the Internet. I found it intimidating and deeply disturbing that Amir would use his ties to the local authorities to obtain my number. I felt horrified, threatened and angry at the same time. Suddenly Akmat's threat that I might be abducted by a Central Asian man during my fieldwork felt real. The fact that during the last 48 hours of my stay, Amir continued to call and text me on WhatsApp, Facebook, Twitter and Instagram, left me in a constant state of fear that Amir would find and abduct me. After inquiring with my female colleagues in the city about their experiences with stalking, I decided to set up a safety protocol with my partner in Switzerland and two local women who agreed to stay up late and wait for my text message that I had arrived at the airport. Luckily, everything went well, and I made it safely back to Switzerland. Even long after I had left the country,

Amir kept on calling and texting me, so that I felt forced to block his phone number. Unfortunately, this did not ward off Amir.

On March 8, 2023, I was awoken by a text message from Amir, who had gotten himself a Swiss phone number to send me an image of flowers for international women's day on WhatsApp. I was terrified. Why and how did he obtain a Swiss number? Was he looking for me in Switzerland? What could he, as a married man with two kids, possibly want from me? A female Central Asian colleague who I contacted for help, was outraged by Amir's behaviour. She argued that, as a woman of the same ethnic group, she could make Amir's stalking public and shame him on Twitter so that his wife and family learned about his shameful demeanour. According to her, "Central Asian men tend to be scared of such kind of publicity". However, we both came to the conclusion that, unfortunately, public "shaming" would not have the intended effect, because I was a foreign woman. Thus, I was not protected by the Central Asian regulative framework of shame (Thibault & Caron, 2022). I decided to turn to my own authorities for help. Unlike in some neighbouring countries, cyberstalking does not constitute a criminal offence in its own right in Switzerland (Stadt Zürich, 2023). Instead, victims are asked to tell the stalker in front of witnesses that they wish to have no contact and to inform their friends and loved ones about the stalker. If the stalking does not cease or worsens, the victim may contact the police. All this is problematic because it suggests that only after Amir attacks me physically, will I be able to get help from my own authorities in Switzerland. Until then, he can continue to follow me around and stalk me online as it pleases him.

While the scholarly literature focussing on sexual harassment of women scholars is growing, little attention has been paid to the implications of cyber harassment on female researchers (Veletsianos et al., 2018). What I found most distressing was the fact that Amir continued to harass me through the Internet and on social media long after I had returned to Switzerland. His call and message from a Swiss number made me realise that I could delete and block his number, but that this would not prevent him or any other person from using another phone number or from creating a new profile to follow my travel and research updates on my public social media accounts in the future. While we as scholars are regularly encouraged to engage in public and in networked scholarship on social media, cyberstalking highlights the potential and far-reaching consequences that any researcher, but especially women, experience when they have a public social media profile.

In the light of the recurrent online harassment, I am wondering if and when I will be able to safely travel to the region in the near future. Due to Amir's ruthless advances, I have had to postpone my planned field trips and to turn down invitations to speak at conference venues in Central Asia. Cyberstalking does not only have a negative impact on a researcher's emotional and physical safety, it also harms their professional career in academia. Early-career female scholars, in particular, are confronted with the paradox of hiding themselves in situations where they are professionally assessed according to their on- and offline visibility as well as the impact factor of their publications. Any form of harassment acts to silence and marginalise female scholars' voices and adversely impacts not just their personal and professional life but also the wider public's access to female scholarship.

Conclusion

As I have tried to show in this essay, even when we, as young foreign female researchers, decide to wear an engagement ring and to dress modestly, unwanted sexual advances by men in the field cannot be precluded. We may belong to a so-called "third sex" (Schwedler, 2006, 425) that grants us easy access to both female and male social circles, but this category does not protect us from sexual harassment. In contrast to local women, neither are our encounters with men regulated by local gender behaviour rules, nor can we make use of the Central Asian cultural mentality of "shame" to ward off potential harassers. Moreover, harassment does not necessarily stop with the end of fieldwork. It can continue in the form of cyberstalking and can take an emotional toll on the researcher. In this context, writing about my encounters with sexual harassment both on- and offline, certainly helped me to cope with the symptoms of "post-traumatic stress disorder" (Pollard, 2009, 3). In addition, I decided to speak out against my stalker and talk about my personal experience with cyberstalking on Twitter:

> Today I woke up by text from my stalker who got himself a new number to send me flowers for #WomensDay on WhatsApp. So thoughtful of him, right? #AcademicTwitter, we need to talk about the consequences of #cyberstalking for women scholars doing #fieldwork! (@jazzdallagnola, March 8, 2023).

To avoid any lawsuit, I did not make my stalker's real name public. Nevertheless, my tweet seems to have struck a chord. It was widely shared and encouraged other female academics to share their own experiences of sexual and cyber harassment. The commentors uniformly agreed that any form of harassment, whether on- or offline should never be tolerated, and therefore, the existing laws need to be toughened. In contrast to previous scholarships' assumption that women who dare to speak out online against misogyny are bullied and silenced (Are, 2020), I did not receive any negative feedback or comments about my tweet. Not even from Amir, who of course, continues to follow my updates on Twitter.

References

Abdullaeva, M. (2021, March 17). 'It happens every day, to everyone': Street harassment in Uzbekistan. *The Diplomat*. https://thediplomat.com/2021/03/it-happens-every-day-to-eve ryone-street-harassment-in-uzbekistan/

Amnesty International Switzerland. (2019). *Sexuelle Belästigung und sexuelle Gewalt an Frauen sind in der Schweiz verbreitet*. Accessed on 21 March 2023 at https://cockpit.gfsbern.ch/de/coc kpit/sexuelle-gewalt-in-der-schweiz

Are, C. (2020). How Instagram's algorithm is censoring women and vulnerable users but helping online abusers. *Feminist Media Studies, 20*(5), 741–744. https://doi.org/10.1080/14680777. 2020.1783805

Congdon, V. (2015). The 'lone female researcher': Isolation and safety upon arrival in the field. *Journal of the Anthropological Society of Oxford, 7*(1), 15–24.

Dall'Agnola, J. (2022). 'Tell me sister'—Social media, a tool for women activists in Tajikistan. *Central Asian Affairs, 9*(1), 119–147. https://doi.org/10.30965/22142290-12340018

Kulakhmetova, A., & Zhailau, Y. (2022, June 30). 'Don't be shy'—Kazakh girls fight sexual harassment. *EurasiaNet*. https://eurasianet.org/dont-be-shy-kazakh-girls-fight-sexual-harassment

Moreno, E. (1995). Rape in the field: Reflections from a survivor. In D. Kulick & M. Willson (Eds.), *Taboo: Sex, identity, and erotic subjectivity in anthropological fieldwork* (pp. 219–250). Routledge.

Peinhopf, A. (2023). Understanding and managing one's own mistrust. In J. Dall'Agnola, A. Edwards, & M. Howlett (Eds.), *Researching the former Soviet Union. Stories from the field* (pp. 19–36). Routledge. https://doi.org/10.4324/9781003144168-3

Pollard, A. (2009). Field of screams: Difficulty and ethnographic fieldwork. *Anthropology Matters, 11*(9), 1–24. https://doi.org/10.22582/am.v11i2.10

Schwedler, J. (2006). The third gender: Western female researchers in the Middle East. *Political Science & Politics, 39*(3), 425–428. https://doi.org/10.1017/S104909650606077X

Stadt Zürich. (2023). *Cyber-stalking*. Accessed on 21 March 2023 at https://www.stadt-zuerich.ch/pd/de/index/stadtpolizei_zuerich/praevention/digitale-medien/grauzone-oder-strafbare-aktivitaet/cyber-stalking.html

Thibault, H. (2021). 'Are You married?': Gender and faith in political ethnographic research. *Journal of Contemporary Ethnography, 50*(3), 395–416. https://doi.org/10.1177/0891241620986852

Thibault, H., & Caron, J. (2022). *Uyat and the culture of shame in Central Asia*. Palgrave Macmillan Singapore. https://doi.org/10.1007/978-981-19-4328-7

Veletsianos, G., Houlden, S., Hodson, J., & Gosse, C. (2018). Women scholars' experiences with online harassment and abuse: Self-protection, resistance, acceptance, and self-blame. *New Media & Society, 20*(12), 4689–4708. https://doi.org/10.1177/1461444818781324

Jasmin Dall'Agnola is a postdoctoral scholar at the George Washington University's Elliott School of International Affairs Institute for European, Russian, and Eurasian Studies. She holds a Ph.D. in Politics and International Relations from Oxford Brookes University. Her research focuses on the relationship between technology, surveillance and governance in authoritarian societies. Her research has been published by numerous peer-reviewed academic journals, including *Europe-Asia Studies, Religions, Central Asian Affairs, Central Asian Survey, and Surveillance & Society*. She is the lead editor of the book *Researching the Former Soviet Union: Stories From the Field* (Routledge, 2023).

Open Access This chapter is licensed under the terms of the Creative Commons Attribution 4.0 International License (http://creativecommons.org/licenses/by/4.0/), which permits use, sharing, adaptation, distribution and reproduction in any medium or format, as long as you give appropriate credit to the original author(s) and the source, provide a link to the Creative Commons license and indicate if changes were made.

The images or other third party material in this chapter are included in the chapter's Creative Commons license, unless indicated otherwise in a credit line to the material. If material is not included in the chapter's Creative Commons license and your intended use is not permitted by statutory regulation or exceeds the permitted use, you will need to obtain permission directly from the copyright holder.

MIX
Papier aus verantwortungsvollen Quellen
Paper from responsible sources
FSC® C105338

If you have any concerns about our products,
you can contact us on
ProductSafety@springernature.com

In case Publisher is established outside the EU,
the EU authorized representative is:
**Springer Nature Customer Service Center GmbH
Europaplatz 3, 69115 Heidelberg, Germany**

Printed by Libri Plureos GmbH
in Hamburg, Germany